MW01257966

SAMUEL JOHNSON ON LITERATURE

MILESTONES OF THOUGHT

SAMUEL JOHNSON ON LITERATURE

Edited and with an Introduction by
Marlies K. Danziger

FREDERICK UNGAR PUBLISHING CO.
NEW YORK

Printed in the United States of America

Design by Anita Duncan

Library of Congress Cataloging in Publication Data

Johnson, Samuel, 1709–1784.
Samuel Johnson on literature.

(Milestones of thought)
Bibliography: p.
1. Literature–Collected works. 2. English literature—History and criticism—Collected works. I. Danzinger, Marlies K. II. Title. III. Title: On literature. IV. Series: Milestones of thought in the history of ideas.
PR3523.D36 820′.9 78-20936
ISBN 0-8044-6097-3

CONTENTS

INTRODUCTION

"The delight of tragedy proceeds from the consciousness of fiction; if we thought murders and treasons real, they would please no more." "The stream of time, which is continually washing the dissoluble fabrics of other poets, passes without injury the adamant of Shakespeare." "Why, Sir, if you read Richardson for the story, your impatience would be so much fretted that you would hang yourself. But you must read him for the sentiment. . . ." The pseudo-primitive epics of Ossian could have been written not just by any modern man but "by many men, many women, and many children."[1] The voice of Samuel Johnson (1709–1784), succinctly formulating complex ideas, firmly praising or debunking other writers, still sounds as forceful—as eloquent or caustic—today as it must have done two hundred years ago.

Writing about literature from the 1750s to the 1780s, Johnson was the last great spokesman for classical or neoclassical values in eighteenth-century England. Working at a time when sentimentalism, soon to become romanticism, was already in vogue, he vigorously tried to maintain what he considered saner and more reasonable standards. What makes Johnson fascinating is not, however, merely his historical position but rather the fact that he took very little for granted. He rethought long-accepted principles and reconsidered seemingly well-established literary reputations, always testing these by his own

[1] From the *Preface to Shakespeare* and *Boswell's Life of Johnson;* each of these quotations appears in its context in the anthology section.

experience and irrepressible common sense. Moreover, he formulated his conclusions in trenchant, pithy terms that have made him one of the most frequently quoted critics in the English language. Whether one agrees or disagrees with his pronouncements, one can count on Johnson for thought-provoking literary judgments.

This brief anthology is intended to suggest the range of Johnson's thoughts about literature. The selections from Johnson's own periodical *The Rambler* (1750–51) and from *The Adventurer* (1753–54) show his interest in such topics as literature and morality; the traditional genres of the pastoral, tragedy, and comedy; the classical rules for drama; the language of poetry; and literary imitation as distinct from plagiarism. Chapter X of the philosophical tale *Rasselas* (1759) expresses his belief in the mission of the poet in idealized terms, slightly undercut by the ironic beginning of Chapter XI.

The Preface to *The Plays of William Shakespeare,* known as the *Preface to Shakespeare* (1765) and written for the edition of Shakespeare's plays that occupied Johnson from 1756 to 1765, weighs the dramatist's strengths and weaknesses and also reevaluates the classical rules for drama in the light of the spectator's actual experience in the theater. The *Notes* for this edition include perceptive character sketches of some of Shakespeare's most complex figures.

The sampling from the *Prefaces, Biographical and Critical, of the Works of the English Poets,* known as the *Lives of the Poets* (1779–81), shows Johnson's frequently caustic commentary and succinct evaluations of specific works. (Because of their length, none of the biographical portions could be included here, and the critical portions of only four of the most important *Lives* could be reproduced.) The passages from James Boswell's *Life of Johnson* (1791), finally, give Johnson's opinions of various literary figures, especially of his contemporaries, and often show him at his most pungent.

To do justice to Johnson's ideas about literature, we must bear in mind that apart from being endowed with his well-known common sense and practicality, he was also an idealist. He had the highest expectations of the writer, describing a poet as "the interpreter of nature and the legislator of mankind" (*Rasselas,* Ch. X) and declaring that "it is always a writer's duty to make the world better" (*Preface to Shakespeare*). Many of Johnson's comments on individual writers are so sharply critical because he was judging them by almost unattainable standards.

Furthermore, we must beware of taking Johnson's remarks out of context or accepting the part for the whole. If we remember the famous statement, in a passage on the flaws of *Paradise Lost,* that it is "one of the books the reader admires and lays down and forgets to take up again. None ever wished it longer than it is," we should also remember that earlier in the *Life of Milton,* in the passage on the beauties of the poem, Johnson found it one of the greatest productions of the human mind, second only to Homer's *Iliad.*

In focusing on the writer's strengths and weaknesses, Johnson was following the accepted critical practices of his day. He himself had defined a critic as "A man skilled in the art of judging literature; a man able to distinguish the faults and beauties of writing,"[2] and he liked to arrive at definitive judgments of the writings he considered. As basis for such judgments, he adopted and rethought several of the principles of neoclassicism that were the heritage of the preceding centuries.

The most fundamental of these principles, and one that pervaded Johnson's thinking about literature, was the Aristotelian concept of imitation. At a time when poetry was coming to be regarded as a form of personal expression and when Shakespeare, in particular, was being praised for the outpourings of his creative genius, Johnson still saw Shakespeare as the poet who imitates reality, who—in the popular image for imitation—"holds up to his readers a faithful mirror of manners and of life." However, Johnson reformulated the concept of imitation by declaring that literature should imitate or represent "general nature": "Nothing can please many and please long but just representations of general nature" (*Preface*).

Just what Johnson meant by "general nature" has been much debated by modern scholars. Is it a reflection of the Platonic ideal, or is it the empiricist philosophers' general category, determined by studying many particulars?[3] The context suggests the latter interpretation. When Johnson praised Shakespeare for making his characters timeless and universal—"the genuine progeny of common humanity,

---

[2] "Critick," *Dictionary of the English Language,* quoted in Jean H. Hagstrum, *Samuel Johnson's Literary Criticism* (Minneapolis, 1952), p. 24.

[3] See W. K. Wimsatt, Jr., and Cleanth Brooks, *Literary Criticism: A Short History* (New York, 1964), pp. 331–33; Leopold Damrosch, Jr., *The Uses of Johnson's Criticism* (Charlottesville, 1976), p. 23 ff; Donald J. Greene, *Samuel Johnson* (New York, 1970), p. 200 ff.

such as the world will always supply and observation will always find"—he recognized that Shakespeare was drawing on "observation" of specific cases and an extensive knowledge of "the world."

Indeed, Johnson was primarily expanding on the idea, widely held in his day, that literature should deal with the typical—with traits observable in many cases—rather than with the merely individual, special, or singular. Shakespeare went beyond other playwrights, Johnson argued, by representing not just national or professional types but still more universal characters: "His persons act and speak by the influence of those general passions and principles by which all minds are agitated. . . ." Johnson's interest in universal characters is seen again in his praise of the novelist Samuel Richardson's "characters of nature"—unchanging moral or psychological types—which Johnson contrasted with Henry Fielding's "characters of manners"—mere social types likely to differ from age to age (Boswell's *Life*).

Johnson favored the general not only in the characterization of plays or novels but also in descriptive poetry. In a much-quoted passage from *Rasselas,* Johnson had the philosopher Imlac declare that a poet is

> to examine not the individual but the species, to remark general properties and large appearances; he does not number the streaks of the tulip or describe the different shades in the verdure of the forest. He is to exhibit in his portraits of nature such prominent and striking features as recall the original to every mind. . . .
>
> (Ch. X)

This statement does not mean, as is sometimes thought, that Johnson disapproved of concrete descriptions and preferred abstract generalities. The reference to "prominent and striking features" shows that he welcomed a few well-chosen specific details provided they did not detract from the universality of the description. His main concern was with the general in the sense of the universal.

Behind this insistence on the general was the conviction, which Johnson shared with other neoclassical writers, that human nature remains fundamentally unchanged through the ages. He believed strongly that literature could and should remind readers of what they already know, and that they know a great deal because of the common experiences of mankind. He was also convinced that reasonable people of all periods could agree in their judgments of literature because of their common experiences. Significantly, Johnson had great faith in the so-called test of time. When he acclaimed Shakespeare for having withstood this test, Johnson was not bowing to the authority of earlier critics; rather, he considered it a sign of excellence if a literary work had survived the prejudices of its own time and the scrutiny of later generations. And he was interested in the verdict not of literary specialists but of "the common reader" (*Life of Gray*), by which he meant unprejudiced, reasonable, literate people.

Johnson realized that his views precluded great novelty or originality. In *The Adventurer,* No. 95, he emphasized that great truths have presumably been recognized and formulated long ago, and that writers who repeat them are not to be considered guilty of plagiarism. His main objection to the metaphysical poets of the early seventeenth century was that they were, as he saw it, perversely industrious in seeking out unfamiliar and correspondingly far-fetched ideas or images (*Life of Cowley*). The only kind of originality Johnson admired—at a time when original genius was already much discussed[4]—was the unexpected expression of ideas one recognizes to be true even if one has not thought of them oneself. Johnson's praise of Thomas Gray's "Elegy Written in a Country Churchyard" is revealing; he finds some of the stanzas "to me original: I have never seen the notions in any other place; yet he that reads them here persuades himself that he has always felt them" (*Life of Gray*).

Another distinctly neoclassical idea that Johnson took very seriously was Horace's dictum that poetry should both instruct and delight. Intensely interested in morality in every aspect of life, Johnson consistently emphasized the element of instruction in literature. He warned against the dangers of immorality in the newly popular realistic novels since these imitate ordinary life that is familiar to their readers and might mislead them, especially if they are young and inexperienced (*The Rambler,* No. 4). He objected to Shakespeare's

---

[4] E.g. in Edward Young, *Conjectures on Original Composition* (1759). See Rene Wellek, *A History of Modern Criticism,* Vol. I (New Haven, 1955), pp. 109–10; John Wain, Introduction, *Johnson as Critic* (London, 1973), p. 13.

inattention to poetic justice—his failure to reward the good and punish the wicked in accordance with an ideal standard of justice (*Preface*)—and was deeply troubled by the undeserved deaths of Cordelia and Ophelia (*Notes* on *King Lear* and on *Hamlet*). Moreover, he reflected at great length on the moral issues raised in *Paradise Lost* with its focus on the fundamental experiences of mankind's fall and redemption (*Life of Milton*).

While emphasizing the need to instruct, Johnson also took seriously the need to please. "That book is good in vain which the reader throws away," he wrote in his *Life of Dryden*. "He only is the master who keeps the mind in pleasing captivity, whose pages are perused with eagerness, and in hope of new pleasure are perused again, and whose conclusion is perceived with an eye of sorrow such as the traveler casts upon departing day." Johnson defended Alexander Pope for adding unHomeric touches to his translation of the *Iliad* with the argument that a writer's first concern is to please his audience and make sure he is read. Furthermore, Johnson fully realized that to instruct without pleasing is futile. His final comment on Milton's *Comus* was that it is "tediously instructive"—clearly a negative verdict (*Life of Milton*).

When Johnson found certain widely accepted neoclassical principles contrary to actual experience, however, he did not hesitate to reject them. He questioned the critics' right to establish "rules" for literature (*The Rambler,* No. 158), and he found the so-called rules of classical drama untenable when tested against what Shakespeare, who disregarded them, accomplished with such brilliant results. Not that a questioning of the rules is in itself contrary to neoclassicism, since great writers were always considered at liberty to go their own way,[5] but Johnson was certainly opposing the views of a number of more narrowly prescriptive critics of his own time, including Voltaire.

Shakespeare's inclusion of comic material in his tragedies and of tragic material in his comedies—a violation of the widely accepted principle that tragedy should restrict itself to tragic incidents and comedy to comic—was firmly defended by Johnson. He recognized that a mingling of the tragic and the comic is actually closer to "the

[5] Bertrand H. Bronson, Introduction, *Johnson on Shakespeare,* ed. Arthur Sherbo, Vol. I (New Haven, 1968), pp. xxviii–ix.

appearance of life" than a strict separation of the two. Besides, he argued, the very change of mood may be pleasing, since spectators like variety. In short, Johnson focused not on any critic-made rules but rather on the actual experience of the audience, himself included.

Again drawing on actual experience, Johnson strongly defended Shakespeare's disregard of the classical unities of time and place. In one of his most brilliant insights inspired by common sense, Johnson pointed out that if spectators can take—or mistake—the stage for any geographical place and the time of the action for any time other than their own, they can just as well accept changes of place and lapses in time during the course of the action. Mocking the assumption that a spectator watching *Anthony and Cleopatra* really "believes that his walk to the theater has been a voyage to Egypt," Johnson argued ironically:

> Surely he that imagines this may imagine more. He that can take the stage at one time for the palace of the Ptolemies may take it in half an hour for the promontory of Actium. Delusion, if delusion be admitted, has no certain limitation.
>
> (*Preface*)

But Johnson did not consider the theatrical experience a "delusion" as some of his contemporaries did[6]; rather, he insisted that "the spectators are always in their senses" and are aware of the fact that they are watching a specific performance—"that the stage is only a stage and that the players are only players." To emphasize the point, he maintained that the spectators really come to the theater primarily "to hear a certain number of lines recited with just gesture and elegant modulation"; that is, to see people known to be actors show their skill in what is known to be only a performance.

Johnson did, however, face the question of how drama can move the passions if spectators do not believe in the action of the play. He answered this question by returning to the principle of literature as imitation. "It [drama] is credited with all the credit due to a drama. It is credited, whenever it moves, as a just picture of a real original, as representing to the auditor what he would himself feel if he were to do

[6] E.g. Henry Home, Lord Kames, *Elements of Criticism* (1762), with his theory of "ideal presence."

or suffer what is there feigned. . . ." But Johnson insisted that apart from this hypothetical identification, some awareness of "fiction" is an important part of the spectators' experience, for they would not be pleased at all if they took the murders or treasons shown on stage to be real. In trying to define the audience's distinctive experience—an experience somewhere between total illusion on the one hand and unremitting consciousness of declaimed speeches on the other, Johnson contributed to the growing awareness in the eighteenth century of the special nature of the aesthetic experience.

In one respect Johnson seems to have departed altogether from traditional neoclassicism. His work on the Shakespeare edition led him to recognize the importance of the historical context of a literary work. As he declared in his *Preface,* "Every man's performance, to be rightly estimated, must be compared with the state of the age in which he lived and with his particular opportunities." Johnson explained Shakespeare's inclusion of the strange and marvelous—the witches in *Macbeth,* for instance—as well as the wealth of incidents and "the shows and bustle in which his plays abound" in terms of the Elizabethan audience's unrefined taste. And he tried to account for the excesses in Lear's behavior in terms of "the barbarity and ignorance" of the age in which Lear supposedly lived (*Notes* on *King Lear*). This historical perspective did not, however, prevent Johnson from ultimately judging Shakespeare and indeed the other writers who interested him in accordance with unchanging, universal standards.[7]

Johnson's historical sense also led him to have definite ideas about the development of English poetry. He believed, for instance, that the diction of English poetry had progressed from the roughness and archaicisms of Edmund Spenser, through the "quibbles," or puns, and inappropriately "low" words of Shakespeare and through the far-fetched images of the metaphysical poets to the increasing smoothness and simplicity of Dryden and Pope. Even though he could not resist mentioning the flaws of many individual poems by Pope, he regarded Pope's work as the height of poetic achievement and eloquently described it as "always smooth, uniform, and gentle . . . a velvet lawn, shaven by the scythe and leveled by the roller" (*Life of Pope*).

Moreover, Johnson was sure that rhyme was the most appropriate form for English poetry and did not hesitate to criticize Shake-

[7] Wellek, pp. 101–04.

speare, Milton, and others for choosing blank verse (unrhymed pentameter). All these opinions suggest that Johnson's taste in poetry was strongly influenced by the neoclassicism that dominated English art and letters in the late seventeenth and early eighteenth century, a generation or two before Johnson's own.

Because of his pronounced taste, Johnson was far from sympathetic to the newest literary trends of his day. He found Gray's effusive Pindaric odes, much admired by his contemporaries, needlessly pretentious—"forced plants raised in a hot-bed"—and considered the experimental novel *Tristram Shandy* too odd to survive. He particularly disliked the cult of primitivism that was becoming fashionable. His scholarly instincts and sound common sense made him steadfastly refuse to accept the authenticity of the supposedly primitive epics of the Celtic bard Ossian, actually the fabrications of the young Scotsman James Macpherson. And Johnson thought Rousseau's paradoxical defense of primitive life a ridiculous search for novelty, not to be believed when tested by experience, and probably, Johnson suggested, not even believed by Rousseau himself (Boswell's *Life*). On the other hand, Johnson fully appreciated those of his contemporaries who upheld good sense and wit in their works, notably Goldsmith and Sheridan.

To what extent, we may now ask, can we as modern readers still agree with Johnson's premises and judgments? Some of the conclusions that he considered virtually self-evident we are bound to question and are likely to accept only partially, if at all. Chief among these is Johnson's emphasis on the general, particularly in relation to Shakespeare, since we tend to admire highly individualized characters and to consider especially Shakespeare's complex figures as such. Still, even if we do not accept Johnson's exclusive emphasis on the general, we are reminded by him that the greatest literary characters, for all their individuality, also have a universal quality. Moreover, Johnson's open didacticism—his insistence that literature offer instruction and his disapproval of any possible undermining of strict morality—is no longer acceptable to modern readers. And yet it is refreshing to see literature viewed with the highest seriousness by a writer who weighs all of life in moral terms.

As for Johnson's ideas about poetic style—about prosody and imagery—we are also likely to question some of these. We would not agree that rhyme is preferable to blank verse, nor that puns and word play are detrimental to poetry. However much we may admire Dryden and Pope, we probably do not regard them as unsurpassed in poetic achievement.

Yet other insights of Johnson's about poetry sound remarkably modern. For instance, he questioned the widespread belief that the sound should echo the sense, pointing out that very few words can, in fact, do so (*Life of Pope*). And he distrusted pretentious poetic diction, preferring—in theory, even if not in his own poems—a vocabulary and word order closer to normal speech (*Life of Milton*). As he put it amusingly in his *Life of Collins*: "He affected the obsolete when it was not worthy of revival, and he put his words out of the common order, seeming to think, with some later candidates for fame, that not to write prose is certainly to write poetry."

Occasionally, Johnson takes us aback by pronouncements that seem amazingly simplistic—as if his practicality led him to an odd sort of literalism. And although many of Johnson's literalisms cannot be taken quite literally—they are part of his polemical attack—some of them he seems really to have meant.

In particular, Johnson sometimes wrote about the concept of imitation as if this meant an accurate copy of life—the more literally true, the better. He assumed that the readers of realistic novels would compare the fictional characters with known originals and would be displeased by "any deviation from exactness of resemblance" (*The Rambler,* No. 4). He found Pope's *Eloisa to Abelard* deeply moving because the characters are known to have actually lived and "the heart naturally loves truth" (*Life of Pope*).

In his notorious condemnation of Milton's *Lycidas,* Johnson again apparently valued literal truthfulness when he objected that Milton and the drowned Edward King who is being eulogized never actually cultivated fields or tended sheep together. More importantly, Johnson also insisted on emotional truthfulness or sincerity, complaining that *Lycidas* "is not to be considered the effusion of real passion. . . . Passion plucks no berries from the myrtle and ivy, nor calls upon Arethuse and Mincius. . . . Where there is leisure for fiction there is little grief" (*Life of Milton*). In expecting a deep personal involvement on the part of the poet, Johnson ignored the importance of craftsmanship and literary convention, and he even, as critics have recently pointed out, contradicted his earlier insistence that being aware of the "fiction" is an important part of the aesthetic experience.[8] The attack on *Lycidas* is sometimes interpreted as a prefiguring of the romantic concern with the poet's emotions, but on the whole, Johnson did not approve of such effusions. His criticism of the poem probably reflects, rather, Johnson's general dislike of pastoral conventions, which he found outworn and archaic (*The Rambler,* No. 37).

Finally, Johnson was amazingly literal-minded about allegorical and otherwise symbolic figures. He reduced the plot of *Comus* to absurdity by describing the symbolic actions of the allegorical characters as if these were functioning in the real world. In a more serious vein, he severely criticized the figures of Sin and Death in *Paradise Lost* because they take a greater part in the poem's action than Johnson thought appropriate for mere extended personifications (*Life of Milton*). Johnson's lack of interest in and feeling for the symbolic[9] seems strange indeed to modern readers.

With these various limitations, why is Johnson still considered important today? Quite apart from his historical significance as a representative of an eighteenth-century point of view, he is remarkable for his extraordinary grasp of the essential quality of the writers he discussed. Many of his summaries are unforgettable. For instance, he eloquently described Milton's great strength in *Paradise Lost* as "gigantic loftiness" or sublimity—"the power of displaying the vast, illuminating the splendid, enforcing the awful [awe-inspiring], darkening the gloomy, and aggravating the dreadful" (*Life of Milton*). He defined the differences between Dryden and Pope in balanced contrasts that do justice to both poets:

> If the flights of Dryden . . . are higher, Pope continues longer on the wing. If of Dryden's fire the blaze is brighter, of Pope's the heat is more regular and constant. Dryden often surpasses expectation, and Pope never falls below it. Dryden is read with frequent astonishment, and Pope with perpetual delight.
>
> (*Life of Pope*)

Even when we no longer accept Johnson's ultimate judgment—his rejection of metaphysical wit, for example—we find his formulations

---

[8] Paul Fussell, *Samuel Johnson and the Life of Writing* (New York, 1971), pp. 54–55.

[9] Wellek, pp. 82, 97–9.

indispensable. Hardly a single modern study of John Donne or Abraham Cowley fails to quote Johnson's definition of metaphysical wit as "the most heterogeneous ideas . . . yoked by violence together" (*Life of Cowley*).

Furthermore, some of Johnson's formulations reveal him as the master of the slashing put-down, deflating pretentiousness or debunking what he considered overrated works with a satirical skill that is timeless. Crushingly, he questioned Pope's grasp of philosophical and theological concepts in *An Essay on Man:* "Having exalted himself into the chair of wisdom, he tells us much that every man knows and much that he does not know himself . . ." (*Life of Pope*). Elsewhere, Johnson used earthy, commonplace images amusingly incongruous with his subject: cucumbers for Gray's elaborate odes, an eagle and a wren for Richardson's novels and those of the French, "the morals of a whoremaster" for the Earl of Chesterfield's worldly advice to his son (Boswell's *Life*). Here Johnson's literalisms stand him in good stead.

Then, too, Johnson's writings about literature offer unexpected flashes of psychological insight, often the result of his pervasive scepticism about people's behavior or motives. Reflecting on the vanities and erratic behavior of women dramatized in Pope's *Rape of the Lock,* Johnson not only pointed to their destructive effect on family life but also added the startlingly perceptive comment: "It has been well observed that the misery of man proceeds not from any single crush of overwhelming evil but from small vexations continually repeated." Reflecting on Pope's own hurt feelings and threats never to write again after the attacks on *The Dunciad,* Johnson gave his astute judgment: "The man who threatens the world is always ridiculous, for the world can easily go on without him and in a short time will cease to miss him" (*Life of Pope*).

These and similar remarks appear even more poignant if we are aware of the deeply felt experiences that gave rise to them. Modern biographers—notably Walter Jackson Bate and John Wain[10]—have drawn attention to the psychological as well as financial hardships Johnson suffered for many years. Indeed a knowledge of his life helps to clarify his writings about literature—not only some of his ideas but

---

[10] Walter Jackson Bate, *Samuel Johnson* (New York, 1977); John Wain, *Samuel Johnson* (New York, 1974).

also his tone, which at times seems excessively, even irritatingly, authoritative.

It is important to recognize, for instance, that when Johnson turned to literary criticism, he was already in his forties—a mature man, who no doubt felt that he had the experience to make forthright, judicious pronouncements. He had had solid grounding in the classics at school in Lichfield and Stourbridge, and during the one year his father's finances permitted him to study at Oxford. He had read voraciously on his own. He had tried his hand at schoolmastering, and during his first years in London had taken on a series of strenuous but ill-paid writing jobs, struggling to support himself and his wife Tetty.

He first made a name for himself as "Dictionary Johnson," editor of the great *Dictionary of the English Language* (1755), which not only provided definitions of words but also traced their usage in earlier writers. This lexicographical work, which Johnson accomplished with only a few helpers between 1746 and 1755, led him to review the major writers in the English language and also no doubt strengthened his ability to formulate succinct definitions.

Johnson's major literary projects were, like the *Dictionary,* the results of definite assignments. He was under contract for both the Shakespeare edition and the *Lives of the Poets*. Indeed, the *Lives*—fifty-two in all—were written at the special request of a group of London booksellers, and to understand why quite minor poets were included whereas more important ones were omitted, we must realize that the booksellers, not Johnson, made the choice. Usually hard-pressed financially, Johnson liked specific assignments and once declared that "No one but a blockhead ever wrote except for money." In actual fact, he was not so mercenary as this statement sounds and wrote a number of pieces anonymously to help friends in financial straits.[11] He seems, however, to have needed the pressure of deadlines, and even with these he took several years longer on the Shakespeare edition than he had promised.

Altogether, Johnson was a highly complicated man. His down-to-earth practicality and common sense, which have been attributed in part to his English Midlands background,[12] were offset by fits of melancholy and indolence, compulsive behavior, and fear of madness.

---

[11] Bate, p. 334 ff.

[12] John Wain, Introduction, *Johnson as Critic* (London, 1973), p. 6.

He is now thought to have experienced two or three nervous breakdowns.[13] He seems to have been beset constantly by feelings of guilt and to have struggled to overcome what he considered his weaknesses.

It was probably at least in part to counteract these problems that Johnson laid so much emphasis on ethical principles—principles that guided his life and pervaded his writings. Johnson's ethics were buttressed by his religious beliefs as an Anglican, a member of the established Church of England comparable to an American Episcopalian. As might be expected, Johnson did not merely accept the teachings of his religion but rather tried fully to understand and actively to live by them. As a young man, he was profoundly influenced by William Law's *A Serious Call to a Devout and Holy Life* (1728), a treatise that set high, almost unattainable standards for the practicing Christian.[14] Throughout his life, Johnson expressed his religious feelings in personal prayers and meditations, some of which have survived.

Johnson's major literary works show his enduring interest in moral predicaments seen in the light of religious principles. His most important poem, *The Vanity of Human Wishes* (1749), dramatizes the futility of pursuing wealth or fame and ends with a Stoic acceptance of human limitations as well as with the Christian advice that only if one cultivates charity, patience, and faith, can one "*make* the happiness" one does not find on earth. The philosophical tale *Rasselas* ridicules the major characters' futile attempts to make a satisfying "choice of life" and again illustrates the vanity of human wishes. Both the poem and the tale reflect Johnson's conviction that literature should instruct as well as delight.

Not only this general belief in the didactic function of literature but also some of his specific literary judgments reveal the influence of Johnson's moral and religious principles. It is surely no accident that so much of the *Life of Milton* is devoted to *Paradise Lost* and in particular to weighing Milton's ability to write about what Johnson considered the supreme religious truths. Quite possibly, too, the negative appraisal of Pope's *Essay on Man* was due to Johnson's painful

---

[13] Bate, pp. 115–29, 342 ff, 371–9, 407–12.

[14] Chester F. Chapin, *The Religious Thought of Samuel Johnson* (Ann Arbor, 1968), pp. 38–40.

awareness of human misery and his feeling that Pope's summary of the traditional arguments did not adequately explain why evil exists in the universe. Certainly Johnson's own moral and religious position accounts for his strong disapproval of Rousseau, notorious for his unconventional personal life and unorthodox religious beliefs, and of Voltaire, equally notorious for his iconoclasm and outspoken attacks on religious institutions. It is noteworthy that although Johnson belongs to the Enlightenment in his interest in reason and the spread of knowledge, he differs from many of the Continental representatives of the Enlightenment precisely in retaining orthodox moral and religious ideas.

In his lighter moments, Johnson was not averse to companionship and sociability. He formed close friendships—among others, with the admiring young Scotsman James Boswell, whom he met in 1763. Furthermore, Johnson became a founding member of several clubs at various stages in his life, notably of the Literary Club, begun in 1764 and continuing its lively dinner meetings into the 1780s. Its membership included Sir Joshua Reynolds, Oliver Goldsmith, Edmund Burke, and, later, David Garrick, Boswell, Edward Gibbon, and Richard Brinsley Sheridan. Such social occasions, as well as Boswell's more private visits whenever he was in London, inspired the pithy comments on literature recorded in Boswell's *Life*. We must remember, however, that Boswell was less interested in recreating the flow of actual conversations than in capturing his respected friend's very best remarks—a fact that no doubt contributed to their wit and brevity.

Increasingly, during his mature life, Johnson took pride in making a career for himself as a professional man of letters. He accepted a modest government pension in 1762, and he was deeply pleased when King George III, at a private meeting in 1767, complimented him on his writings. But he remained fiercely independent from first to last. In commenting on literature, he was not afraid to trust his own good sense more than long accepted rules. He felt quite free to praise or criticize even the most admired writers of England—Shakespeare, Milton, Pope—according to his own lights. And he did not hesitate to ridicule what he considered the passing literary fads of his day. While we can hardly overlook the sometimes overly emphatic, overbearing tone, which Coleridge amusingly called Johnson's "bow-wow manner,"[15] we can surely appreciate his forthright, forceful, sometimes provocative but usually thought-provoking appraisals.

A Note on the Texts

The following editions have served as basis for Johnson's texts: *The Rambler,* 4 vols., London, 1761; *Rasselas,* London, 1759; *The Plays of William Shakespeare,* 10 vols., London, 1778; *Prefaces, Biographical and Critical, to the Works of the English Poets,* 10 vols., London, 1779–81; *Boswell's Life of Johnson,* ed. Chauncey Brewster Tinker, 2 vols., New York, 1933.

Spellings have been Americanized, and the punctuation has been modernized wherever possible.

---

[15] Quoted in *Johnson: The Critical Heritage,* ed. James T. Boulton (New York, 1971), p. 356.

1

THE PERIODICAL ESSAYS (1750–1753)

On the Novel and Morality

Simul et jucunda et idonea dicere vitae
(Horace, *Art of Poetry*)

And join both profit and delight in one.
(Trans. Creech)

The works of fiction with which the present generation seems more particularly delighted are such as exhibit life in its true state, diversified only by accidents that daily happen in the world and influenced by passions and qualities which are really to be found in conversing with mankind.[1]

This kind of writing may be termed, not improperly, the comedy of romance and is to be conducted nearly by the rules of comic poetry. Its province is to bring about natural events by easy means and to keep up curiosity without the help of wonder; it is therefore precluded from the machines and expedients of the heroic romance and can neither employ giants to snatch away a lady from the nuptial rites nor knights to bring her back from captivity; it can neither bewilder its personages in deserts nor lodge them in imaginary castles.

---

[1] Johnson is referring to novels such as Samuel Richardson's *Clarissa* (1747–48), Tobias Smollett's *Roderick Random* (1748), and Henry Fielding's *Tom Jones* (1749).

I remember a remark made by Scaliger upon Pontanus[2] that all his writings are filled with the same images and that if you take from him his lilies and his roses, his satyrs and his dryads, he will have nothing left that can be called poetry. In like manner, almost all the fictions of the last age will vanish if you deprive them of a hermit and a wood, a battle and a shipwreck.

Why this wild strain of imagination found reception so long in polite and learned ages, it is not easy to conceive; but we cannot wonder that while readers could be procured, the authors were willing to continue it; for when a man had by practice gained some fluency of language, he had no further care than to retire to his closet,[3] let loose his invention, and heat his mind with incredibilities; a book was thus produced without fear of criticism, without the toil of study, without knowledge of nature or acquaintance with life.

The task of our present writers is very different; it requires, together with that learning which is to be gained from books, that experience which can never be attained by solitary diligence but must arise from general converse and accurate observation of the living world. Their performances have, as Horace expresses it, *plus oneris, quanto veniae minus,* little indulgence and therefore more difficulty. They are engaged in portraits of which every one knows the original and can detect any deviation from exactness of resemblance. Other writings are safe except from the malice of learning, but these are in danger from every common reader; as the slipper ill executed was censured by a shoemaker who happened to stop in his way at the Venus of Appelles.[4]

But the fear of not being approved as just copiers of human manners is not the most important concern that an author of this sort ought to have before him. These books are written chiefly to the young, the ignorant, and the idle, to whom they serve as lectures of conduct and introductions into life. They are the entertainment of minds unfurnished with ideas and therefore easily susceptible of impressions, not fixed by principles and therefore easily following the

[2] The Italian Renaissance critic Scaliger commented on the poems of Giovanni Pontano.

[3] Small private room or study.

[4] Appelles was famous for his lifelike paintings.

current of fancy, not informed by experience and consequently open to every false suggestion and partial account. . . .

It is justly considered as the greatest excellency of art to imitate nature, but it is necessary to distinguish those parts of nature which are most proper for imitation; greater care is still required in representing life, which is so often discolored by passion or deformed by wickedness. If the world be promiscuously[5] described, I cannot see of what use it can be to read the account, or why it may not be as safe to turn the eye immediately upon mankind as upon a mirror which shows all that presents itself without discrimination.

It is therefore not a sufficient vindication of a character that it is drawn as it appears, for many characters ought never to be drawn, nor of a narrative that the train of events is agreeable to observation and experience, for that observation which is called knowledge of the world will be found much more frequently to make men cunning than good. The purpose of these writings is surely not only to show mankind but to provide that they may be seen hereafter with less hazard: to teach the means of avoiding the snares which are laid by treachery for innocence without infusing any wish for that superiority with which the betrayer flatters his vanity, to give the power of counteracting fraud without the temptation to practice it, to initiate youth by mock encounters in the art of necessary defence, and to increase prudence without impairing virtue.

Many writers, for the sake of following nature, so mingle good and bad qualities in their principal personages that they are both equally conspicuous; and as we accompany them through their adventures with delight and are led by degrees to interest ourselves in their favor, we lose the abhorrence of their faults because they do not hinder our pleasure, or perhaps regard them with some kindness for being united with so much merit.

There have been men indeed splendidly wicked, whose endowments threw a brightness on their crimes and whom scarce any villainy made perfectly detestable because they never could be wholly divested of their excellencies; but such have been in all ages the great corrupters of the world, and their resemblance ought no more to be preserved than the art of murdering without pain. . . .

---

[5] Without discrimination.

In narratives where historical veracity has no place, I cannot discover why there should not be exhibited the most perfect idea of virtue: of virtue not angelical nor above probability (for what we cannot credit, we shall never imitate) but the highest and purest that humanity can reach, which, exercised in such trials as the various revolutions of things shall bring upon it, may, by conquering some calamities and enduring others, teach us what we may hope and what we can perform. Vice, for vice is necessary to be shown, should always disgust, nor should the graces of gaiety or the dignity of courage be so united with it as to reconcile it to the mind. Wherever it appears, it should raise hatred by the malignity of its practices and contempt by the meanness of its stratagems; for while it is supported by either parts or spirit, it will be seldom heartily abhorred. The Roman tyrant was content to be hated if he was but feared, and there are thousands of the readers of romances willing to be thought wicked if they may be allowed to be wits. It is therefore to be steadily inculcated that virtue is the highest proof of understanding and the only solid basis of greatness; and that vice is the natural consequence of narrow thoughts, that it begins in mistake and ends in ignominy.

from *The Rambler,* No. 4 (1750)

On the Pastoral

The facility of treating actions or events in the pastoral style has incited many writers, from whom more judgment might have been expected, to put the sorrow or the joy which the occasion required into the mouth of Daphne or Thyrsis[6]; and as one absurdity must naturally be expected to make way for another, they have written with an utter disregard both of life and nature, and filled their productions with mythological allusions, with incredible fictions, and with sentiments which neither passion nor reason could have dictated since the change which religion has made in the whole system of the world.

from *The Rambler,* No. 37 (1750)

---

[6] Conventional names often used in pastorals.

On the Writer, Criticism, and the Rules

It ought to be the first endeavor of a writer to distinguish nature from custom, or that which is established because it is right from that which is right only because it is established, that he may neither violate essential principles by a desire of novelty nor debar himself from the attainment of beauties within his view by a needless fear of breaking rules which no literary dictator had authority to enact.

from *The Rambler,* No. 156 (1751)

Criticism, though dignified from the earliest age by the labors of men eminent for knowledge and sagacity, and since the revival of polite literature the favorite study of European scholars, has not yet attained the certainty and stability of science. The rules hitherto received are seldom drawn from any settled principle or self-evident postulate, or adapted to the natural and invariable constitution of things, but will be found upon examination the arbitrary edicts of legislators, authorized only by themselves, who, out of various means by which the same end may be attained, selected such as happened to occur to their own reflection and then, by a law which idleness and timidity were too willing to obey, prohibited new experiments of wit, restrained fancy from the indulgence of her innate inclination to hazard and adventure, and condemned all future flights of genius to pursue the path of the Maeonian eagle.[7]

This authority may be more justly opposed as it is apparently derived from them whom they endeavor to control; for we owe few of the rules of writing to the acuteness of critics, who have generally no other merit than that, having read the works of great authors with attention, they have observed the arrangement of their matter or the graces of their expression and then expected honor and reverence for precepts which they never could have invented, so that practice has introduced rules rather than rules have directed practice.

from *The Rambler,* No. 158 (1751)

---

[7] Homer.

On Low Words in Shakespeare

We are all offended by low terms but are not disgusted alike by the same compositions because we do not all agree to censure the same terms as low. No word is naturally or intrinsically meaner than another; our opinion therefore of words as of other things arbitrarily and capriciously established depends wholly upon accident and custom. The cottager thinks those apartments splendid and spacious which an inhabitant of palaces will despise for their inelegance, and to him who has passed most of his hours with the delicate and polite many expressions will seem sordid which another equally acute may hear without offence; but a mean term never fails to displease him to whom it appears mean, as poverty is certainly and invariably despised though he who is poor in the eyes of some may by others be envied for his wealth.

Words become low by the occasions to which they are applied or the general character of them who use them, and the disgust which they produce arises from the revival of those images with which they are commonly united. Thus if in the most solemn discourse a phrase happens to occur which has been successfully employed in some ludicrous narrative, the gravest auditor finds it difficult to refrain from laughter when they who are not prepossessed by the same accidental association are utterly unable to guess the reason of his merriment. Words which convey ideas of dignity in one age are banished from elegant writing or conversation in another because they are in time debased by vulgar mouths and can be no longer heard without the involuntary recollection of unpleasing images.

When Macbeth is confirming himself in the horrid purpose of stabbing his king, he breaks out amidst his emotions into a wish natural to a murderer:

> ——Come, thick night!
> And pall thee in the dunnest smoke of hell,
> That my keen knife see not the wound it makes;
> Nor heav'n peep through the blanket of the dark,
> To cry, Hold! hold!

In this passage is exerted all the force of poetry, that force which calls new powers into being, which embodies sentiment and animates matter; yet perhaps scarce any man now peruses it without some disturbance of his attention from the counteraction of the words to the ideas. What can be more dreadful than to implore the presence of night, invested not in common obscurity but in the smoke of hell? Yet the efficacy of this invocation is destroyed by the insertion of an epithet now seldom heard but in the stable, and *dun*[8] night may come or go without any other notice than contempt.

. . . We cannot surely but sympathise with the horrors of a wretch about to murder his master, his friend, his benefactor, who suspects that the weapon will refuse its office and start back from the breast which he is preparing to violate. Yet this sentiment is weakened by the name of an instrument used by butchers and cooks in the meanest employments; we do not immediately conceive that any crime of importance is to be committed with a *knife*, or who does not at last from the long habit of connecting a knife with sordid offices feel aversion rather than terror?

Macbeth proceeds to wish in the madness of guilt that the inspection of heaven may be intercepted and that he may in the involutions of infernal darkness escape the eye of Providence. This is the utmost extravagance of determined wickedness; yet this is so debased by two unfortunate words that while I endeavor to impress on my reader the energy of the sentiment, I can scarce check my risibility when the expression forces itself upon my mind, for who, without some relaxation of his gravity, can hear of the avengers of guilt "peeping through a blanket"?

from *The Rambler,* No. 168 (1751)

On Literary Imitation as Distinct from Plagiarism

It is often charged upon writers that with all their pretensions to genius and discoveries, they do little more than copy one another, and that compositions intruded upon the world with the pomp of novelty contain only tedious repetitions of common sentiments, or at best

[8] Dingy brown color, associated with horses.

exhibit a transposition of known images and give a new appearance to truth only by some slight difference of dress and decoration.

The allegation of resemblance between authors is indisputably true, but the image of plagiarism which is raised upon it is not to be allowed with equal readiness. A coincidence of sentiment may easily happen without any communication, since there are many occasions in which all reasonable men will nearly think alike. Writers of all ages have had the same sentiments because they have in all ages had the same objects of speculation; the interests and passions, the virtues and vices of mankind, have been diversified in different times only by unessential and casual varieties, and we must therefore expect in the works of all those who attempt to describe them such a likeness as we find in the pictures of the same person drawn in different periods of his life.

from *The Adventurer,* No. 95 (1753)

2

RASSELAS (1759)

X: IMLAC'S HISTORY CONTINUED. A DISSERTATION UPON POETRY

"Wherever I went[1] I found that poetry was considered as the highest learning and regarded with a veneration somewhat approaching to that which man would pay to the angelic nature. And it yet fills me with wonder that in almost all countries the most ancient poets are considered as the best: whether it be that every other kind of knowledge is an acquisition gradually attained and poetry is a gift conferred at once; or that the first poetry of every nation surprised them as a novelty and retained the credit by consent which it received by accident at first; or whether, as the province of poetry is to describe nature and passion, which are always the same, the first writers took possession of the most striking objects for description and the most probable occurrences for fiction, and left nothing to those that followed them but transcription of the same events and new combinations of the same images. Whatever be the reason, it is commonly observed that the early writers are in possession of nature and their followers of art; that the first excel in strength and invention, and the latter in elegance and refinement.

---

[1] The wise Imlac is telling the story of his life. His ideas about poetry are clearly Johnson's own.

"I was desirous to add my name to this illustrious fraternity. I read all the poets of Persia and Arabia, and was able to repeat by memory the volumes that are suspended in the mosque of Mecca. But I soon found that no man was ever great by imitation. My desire of excellence impelled me to transfer my attention to nature and to life. Nature was to be my subject and men to be my auditors: I could never describe what I had not seen; I could not hope to move those with delight or terror whose interests and opinions I did not understand.

"Being now resolved to be a poet, I saw everything with a new purpose; my sphere of attention was suddenly magnified; no kind of knowledge was to be overlooked. I ranged mountains and deserts for images and resemblances, and pictured upon my mind every tree of the forest and flower of the valley. I observed with equal care the crags of the rock and the pinnacles of the palace. Sometimes I wandered along the mazes of the rivulet and sometimes watched the changes of the summer clouds. To a poet nothing can be useless. Whatever is beautiful and whatever is dreadful must be familiar to his imagination; he must be conversant with all that is awfully[2] vast or elegantly little. The plants of the garden, the animals of the wood, the minerals of the earth and meteors of the sky must all concur to store his mind with inexhaustible variety, for every idea is useful for the enforcement or decoration of moral or religious truth, and he who knows most will have most power of diversifying his scenes and of gratifying his reader with remote allusions and unexpected instruction.

"All the appearances of nature I was therefore careful to study, and every country which I have surveyed has contributed something to my poetical powers."

"In so wide a survey," said the prince, "you must surely have left much unobserved. I have lived, till now, within the circuit of these mountains and yet cannot walk abroad without the sight of something which I had never beheld before or never heeded."

"The business of a poet," said Imlac, "is to examine not the individual but the species, to remark general properties and large appearances; he does not number the streaks of the tulip or describe the different shades in the verdure of the forest. He is to exhibit in his

---

[2] Awe-inspiring. Imlac is alluding to the sublime (the grandiose, inspiring wonder) and the beautiful (the well-shaped and pleasing) as defined by eighteenth-century critics.

portraits of nature such prominent and striking features as recall the original to every mind and must neglect the minuter discriminations, which one may have remarked and another have neglected, for those characteristics which are alike obvious to vigilance and carelessness.

"But the knowledge of nature is only half the task of a poet; he must be acquainted likewise with all the modes of life. His character requires that he estimate the happiness and misery of every condition, observe the power of all the passions in all their combinations and trace the changes of the human mind as they are modified by various institutions and accidental influences of climate or custom from the sprightliness of infancy to the despondence of decrepitude. He must divest himself of the prejudices of his age or country; he must consider right and wrong in their abstracted and invariable state; he must disregard present laws and opinions, and rise to general and transcendental truths, which will always be the same; he must therefore content himself with the slow progress of his name, contemn the applause of his own time, and commit his claims to the justice of posterity. He must write as the interpreter of nature and the legislator of mankind, and consider himself as presiding over the thoughts and manners of future generations, as a being superior to time and place.

"His labor is not yet at an end: he must know many languages and many sciences, and, that his style may be worthy of his thoughts, must by incessant practice familiarize to himself every delicacy of speech and grace of harmony."

XI: IMLAC'S NARRATIVE CONTINUED

Imlac now felt the enthusiastic fit and was proceeding to aggrandize[3] his own profession when the prince cried out, "Enough! Thou hast convinced me that no human being can ever be a poet. Proceed with thy narration. . . ."[4]

---

[3] Exalt.

[4] Imlac's subsequent narrative no longer deals with literature.

3

SHAKESPEARE CRITICISM (1765)

PREFACE TO THE PLAYS OF WILLIAM SHAKESPEARE

That praises are without reason lavished on the dead and that the honors due only to excellence are paid to antiquity is a complaint likely to be always continued by those who, being able to add nothing to truth, hope for eminence from the heresies of paradox; or those who, being forced by disappointment upon consolatory expedients, are willing to hope from posterity what the present age refuses and flatter themselves that the regard which is yet denied by envy will be at last bestowed by time.

Antiquity, like every other quality that attracts the notice of mankind, has undoubtedly votaries that reverence it not from reason but from prejudice. Some seem to admire indiscriminately whatever has been long preserved without considering that time has sometimes cooperated with chance; all perhaps are more willing to honor past than present excellence, and the mind contemplates genius through the shades of age as the eye surveys the sun through artificial opacity. The great contention of criticism is to find the faults of the moderns and the beauties of the ancients. While an author is yet living, we estimate his powers by his worst performance, and when he is dead, we rate them by his best.

To works, however, of which the excellence is not absolute and definite but gradual and comparative, to works not raised upon principles demonstrative and scientific but appealing wholly to observation and experience, no other test can be applied than length of duration and continuance of esteem. What mankind have long possessed they have often examined and compared, and if they persist to value the possession, it is because frequent comparisons have confirmed opinion in its favor. As among the works of nature no man can properly call a river deep or a mountain high without the knowledge of many mountains and many rivers, so in the productions of genius nothing can be styled excellent till it has been compared with other works of the same kind. Demonstration immediately displays its power and has nothing to hope or fear from the flux of years, but works tentative and experimental must be estimated by their proportion to the general and collective ability of man as it is discovered in a long succession of endeavors. Of the first building that was raised it might be with certainty determined that it was round or square, but whether it was spacious or lofty must have been referred to time. The Pythagorean scale of numbers[1] was at once discovered to be perfect; but the poems of Homer we yet know not to transcend the common limits of human intelligence but by remarking that nation after nation and century after century has been able to do little more than transpose his incidents, new-name his characters, and paraphrase his sentiments.

The reverence due to writings that have long subsisted arises, therefore, not from any credulous confidence in the superior wisdom of past ages or gloomy persuasion of the degeneracy of mankind but is the consequence of acknowledged and indubitable positions that what has been longest known has been most considered, and what is most considered is best understood.

The poet of whose works I have undertaken the revision[2] may now begin to assume the dignity of an ancient and claim the privilege of established fame and prescriptive veneration. He has long outlived his century, the term commonly fixed as the test of literary merit. Whatever advantages he might once derive from personal allusions,

---

[1] The musical scale interpreted by the Greek philosopher Pythagoras as corresponding to a mathematical formula.

[2] New edition.

local customs, or temporary opinions have for many years been lost; and every topic of merriment or motive of sorrow which the modes of artificial[3] life afforded him now only obscure the scenes which they once illuminated. The effects of favor and competition are at an end; the tradition of his friendships and his enmities have perished; his works support no opinion with arguments nor supply any faction with invectives; they can neither indulge vanity nor gratify malignity, but are read without any other reason than the desire of pleasure and are therefore praised only as pleasure is obtained; yet, thus unassisted by interest[4] or passion, they have passed through variations of taste and changes of manners and, as they devolved from one generation to another, have received new honors at every transmission.

But because human judgment, though it be gradually gaining upon certainty, never becomes infallible, and approbation, though long continued, may yet be only the approbation of prejudice or fashion, it is proper to inquire by what peculiarities of excellence Shakespeare has gained and kept the favor of his countrymen.

Nothing can please many and please long but just representations of general nature. Particular manners can be known to few, and therefore few only can judge how nearly they are copied. The irregular combinations of fanciful invention may delight awhile by that novelty of which the common satiety of life sends us all in quest; but the pleasures of sudden wonder are soon exhausted, and the mind can only repose on the stability of truth.

Shakespeare is above all writers, at least above all modern writers, the poet of nature, the poet that holds up to his readers a faithful mirror of manners and of life. His characters are not modified by the customs of particular places, unpracticed by the rest of the world; by the peculiarities of studies or professions which can operate but upon small numbers; or by the accidents of transient fashions or temporary opinions: they are the genuine progeny of common humanity, such as the world will always supply, and observation will always find. His persons act and speak by the influence of those general passions and principles by which all minds are agitated and the whole system of life is continued in motion. In the writings of

[3] All that is not natural; man-made.

[4] Selfish interests.

other poets a character is too often an individual; in those of Shakespeare it is commonly a species.

It is from this wide extension of design that so much instruction is derived. It is this which fills the plays of Shakespeare with practical axioms and domestic wisdom. It was said of Euripides that every verse was a precept, and it may be said of Shakespeare that from his works may be collected a system of civil and economical prudence. Yet his real power is not shown in the splendor of particular passages but by the progress of his fable[5] and the tenor of his dialogue; and he that tries to recommend him by select quotations will succeed like the pedant in Hierocles, who, when he offered his house for sale, carried a brick in his pocket as a specimen.

It will not easily be imagined how much Shakespeare excels in accommodating his sentiments to real life but by comparing him with other authors. It was observed of the ancient schools of declamation that the more diligently they were frequented, the more was the student disqualified for the world because he found nothing there which he should ever meet in any other place. The same remark may be applied to every stage but that of Shakespeare. The theater, when it is under any other direction, is peopled by such characters as were never seen, conversing in a language which was never heard upon topics which will never arise in the commerce of mankind. But the dialogue of this author is often so evidently determined by the incident which produces it and is pursued with so much ease and simplicity that it seems scarcely to claim the merit of fiction but to have been gleaned by diligent selection out of common conversation and common occurrences.

Upon every other stage the universal agent is love, by whose power all good and evil is distributed and every action quickened or retarded. To bring a lover, a lady, and a rival into the fable; to entangle them in contradictory obligations, perplex them with oppositions of interest, and harass them with violence of desires inconsistent with each other, to make them meet in rapture and part in agony, to fill their mouths with hyperbolical joy and outrageous sorrow, to distress them as nothing human ever was distressed, to deliver them as nothing human ever was delivered, is the business of a modern

[5] Plot.

dramatist. For this, probability is violated, life is misrepresented, and language is depraved. But love is only one of many passions; and as it has no great influence upon the sum of life, it has little operation in the dramas of a poet who caught his ideas from the living world and exhibited only what he saw before him. He knew that any other passion, as it was regular or exorbitant, was a cause of happiness or calamity.

Characters thus ample and general were not easily discriminated and preserved, yet perhaps no poet ever kept his personages more distinct from each other. I will not say with Pope that every speech may be assigned to the proper speaker, because many speeches there are which have nothing characteristical; but perhaps, though some may be equally adapted to every person, it will be difficult to find any that can be properly transferred from the present possessor to another claimant. The choice is right when there is reason for choice.

Other dramatists can only gain attention by hyperbolical or aggravated[6] characters, by fabulous and unexampled excellence or depravity, as the writers of barbarous romances invigorated the reader by a giant and a dwarf; and he that should form his expectations of human affairs from the play or from the tale would be equally deceived. Shakespeare has no heroes; his scenes are occupied only by men, who act and speak as the reader thinks that he should himself have spoken or acted on the same occasion; even where the agency is supernatural, the dialogue is level with life. Other writers disguise the most natural passions and most frequent incidents so that he who contemplates them in the book will not know them in the world; Shakespeare approximates the remote and familiarizes the wonderful; the event which he represents will not happen, but if it were possible, its effects would probably be such as he has assigned; and it may be said that he has not only shown human nature as it acts in real exigencies but as it would be found in trials to which it cannot be exposed.

This, therefore, is the praise of Shakespeare, that his drama is the mirror of life; that he who has mazed[7] his imagination in following the phantoms which other writers raise up before him may here be cured of his delirious ecstasies by reading human sentiments in human

---

[6] Heightened, exaggerated.

[7] Bewildered, perplexed.

language, by scenes from which a hermit may estimate the transactions of the world and a confessor predict the progress of the passions.

His adherence to general nature has exposed him to the censure of critics who form their judgments upon narrower principles. Dennis and Rhymer think his Romans not sufficiently Roman, and Voltaire censures his kings as not completely royal. Dennis is offended that Menenius, a senator of Rome, should play the buffoon, and Voltaire perhaps thinks decency violated when the Danish Usurper is represented as a drunkard. But Shakespeare always makes nature predominate over accident, and if he preserves the essential character is not very careful of distinctions superinduced and adventitious. His story requires Romans or kings, but he thinks only on men. He knew that Rome, like every other city, had men of all dispositions, and wanting a buffoon, he went into the senate-house for that which the senate-house would certainly have afforded him. He was inclined to show an usurper and a murderer not only odious but despicable; he therefore added drunkenness to his other qualities, knowing that kings love wine like other men and that wine exerts its natural power upon kings. These are the petty cavils of petty minds; a poet overlooks the casual distinction of country and condition as a painter, satisfied with the figure, neglects the drapery.

The censure which he has incurred by mixing comic and tragic scenes, as it extends to all his works, deserves more consideration. Let the fact be first stated and then examined.

Shakespeare's plays are not in the rigorous and critical sense either tragedies or comedies but compositions of a distinct kind, exhibiting the real state of sublunary nature which partakes of good and evil, joy and sorrow, mingled with endless variety of proportion and innumerable modes of combination, and expressing the course of the world in which the loss of one is the gain of another, in which at the same time the reveller is hasting to his wine and the mourner burying his friend, in which the malignity of one is sometimes defeated by the frolic of another, and many mischiefs and many benefits are done and hindered without design.

Out of this chaos of mingled purposes and casualties[8] the ancient poets, according to the laws which custom had prescribed, selected

---

[8] Chance occurrences.

some the crimes of men and some their absurdities, some the momentous vicissitudes of life and some the lighter occurrences, some the terrors of distress and some the gaieties of prosperity. Thus rose the two modes of imitation known by the names of *tragedy* and *comedy,* compositions intended to promote different ends by contrary means and considered as so little allied that I do not recollect among the Greeks or Romans a single writer who attempted both.

Shakespeare has united the powers of exciting laughter and sorrow not only in one mind but in one composition. Almost all his plays are divided between serious and ludicrous characters and in the successive evolutions of the design sometimes produce seriousness and sorrow, and sometimes levity and laughter.

That this is a practice contrary to the rules of criticism will be readily allowed, but there is always an appeal open from criticism to nature. The end of writing is to instruct; the end of poetry is to instruct by pleasing. That the mingled drama may convey all the instruction of tragedy or comedy cannot be denied, because it includes both in its alternations of exhibition and approaches nearer than either to the appearance of life by showing how great machinations and slender designs may promote or obviate one another, and the high and low co-operate in the general system by unavoidable concatenation.

It is objected that by this change of scenes the passions are interrupted in their progression and that the principal event, being not advanced by a due gradation of preparatory incidents, wants at last the power to move, which constitutes the perfection of dramatic poetry. This reasoning is so specious[9] that it is received as true even by those who in daily experience feel it to be false. The interchanges of mingled scenes seldom fail to produce the intended vicissitudes of passion. Fiction cannot move so much but that the attention may be easily transferred; and though it must be allowed that pleasing melancholy be sometimes interrupted by unwelcome levity, yet let it be considered likewise that melancholy is often not pleasing and that the disturbance of one man may be the relief of another; that different auditors have different habitudes; and that, upon the whole, all pleasure consists in variety.

---

[9] Plausible.

The players, who in their edition divided our author's works into comedies, histories, and tragedies, seem not to have distinguished the three kinds by any very exact or definite ideas.

An action which ended happily to the principal persons, however serious or distressful through its intermediate incidents, in their opinion constituted a comedy. This idea of a comedy continued long amongst us; and plays were written which, by changing the catastrophe, were tragedies to-day and comedies to-morrow.

Tragedy was not in those times a poem of more general dignity or elevation than comedy; it required only a calamitous conclusion, with which the common criticism of that age was satisfied whatever lighter pleasure it afforded in its progress.

History was a series of actions with no other than chronological succession, independent on each other and without any tendency to introduce or regulate the conclusion. It is not always very nicely distinguished from tragedy. There is not much nearer approach to unity of action in the tragedy of *Antony and Cleopatra* than in the history of *Richard the Second.* But a history might be continued through many plays; as it had no plan, it had no limits.

Through all these denominations of the drama, Shakespeare's mode of composition is the same: an interchange of seriousness and merriment, by which the mind is softened at one time and exhilarated at another. But whatever be his purpose, whether to gladden or depress, or to conduct the story without vehemence or emotion through tracts of easy and familiar dialogue, he never fails to attain his purpose; as he commands us, we laugh or mourn or sit silent with quiet expectation in tranquillity without indifference.

When Shakespeare's plan is understood, most of the criticisms of Rymer and Voltaire vanish away. The play of *Hamlet* is opened without impropriety by two sentinels; Iago bellows at Brabantio's window without injury to the scheme of the play, though in terms which a modern audience would not easily endure; the character of Polonius is seasonable and useful; and the grave-diggers themselves may be heard with applause.

Shakespeare engaged in dramatic poetry with the world open before him; the rules of the ancients were yet known to few; the public judgment was unformed; he had no example of such fame as might force him upon imitation nor critics of such authority as might restrain his extravagance; he therefore indulged his natural disposition, and his disposition, as Rymer has remarked, led him to comedy. In tragedy he often writes with great appearance of toil and study what is written at last with little felicity, but in his comic scenes he seems to produce without labor what no labor can improve. In tragedy he is always struggling after some occasion to be comic, but in comedy he seems to repose or to luxuriate as in a mode of thinking congenial to his nature. In his tragic scenes there is always something wanting, but his comedy often surpasses expectation or desire. His comedy pleases by the thoughts and the language, and his tragedy for the greater part by incident and action. His tragedy seems to be skill, his comedy to be instinct.

The force of his comic scenes has suffered little diminution from the changes made by a century and a half in manners or in words. As his personages act upon principles arising from genuine passion very little modified by particular forms, their pleasures and vexations are communicable to all times and to all places; they are natural and therefore durable; the adventitious peculiarities of personal habits are only superficial dies, bright and pleasing for a little while yet soon fading to a dim tinct without any remains of former lustre; but the discriminations of true passion are the colors of nature; they pervade the whole mass and can only perish with the body that exhibits them. The accidental compositions of heterogeneous modes are dissolved by the chance which combined them, but the uniform simplicity of primitive qualities neither admits increase nor suffers decay. The sand heaped by one flood is scattered by another, but the rock always continues in its place. The stream of time, which is continually washing the dissoluble fabrics of other poets, passes without injury by the adamant of Shakespeare.

If there be, what I believe there is, in every nation a style which never becomes obsolete, a certain mode of phraseology so consonant and congenial to the analogy and principles of its respective language as to remain settled and unaltered, this style is probably to be sought in the common intercourse of life, among those who speak only to be understood without ambition of elegance. The polite are always catching modish innovations, and the learned depart from established forms of speech in hope of finding or making better; those who wish for distinction forsake the vulgar,[10] when the vulgar is right; but there is a

[10] The common or ordinary.

conversation above grossness and below refinement where propriety resides and where this poet seems to have gathered his comic dialogue. He is therefore more agreeable to the ears of the present age than any other author equally remote and among his other excellencies deserves to be studied as one of the original masters of our language.

These observations are to be considered not as unexceptionably constant but as containing general and predominant truth. Shakespeare's familiar dialogue is affirmed to be smooth and clear yet not wholly without ruggedness or difficulty, as a country may be eminently fruitful though it has spots unfit for cultivation; his characters are praised as natural though their sentiments are sometimes forced and their actions improbable, as the earth upon the whole is spherical though its surface is varied with protuberances and cavities.

Shakespeare with his excellencies has likewise faults, and faults sufficient to obscure and overwhelm any other merit. I shall show them in the proportion in which they appear to me without envious malignity or superstitious veneration. No question can be more innocently discussed than a dead poet's pretensions to renown, and little regard is due to that bigotry which sets candor[11] higher than truth.

His first defect is that to which may be imputed most of the evil in books or in men. He sacrifices virtue to convenience and is so much more careful to please than to instruct that he seems to write without any moral purpose. From his writings indeed a system of social duty may be selected, for he that thinks reasonably must think morally; but his precepts and axioms drop casually from him; he makes no just distribution of good or evil nor is always careful to show in the virtuous a disapprobation of the wicked; he carries his persons indifferently through right and wrong, and at the close dismisses them without further care and leaves their examples to operate by chance. This fault the barbarity of his age cannot extenuate, for it is always a writer's duty to make the world better, and justice is a virtue independent on time or place.

The plots are often so loosely formed that a very slight consideration may improve them, and so carelessly pursued that he seems not always fully to comprehend his own design. He omits opportunities of instructing or delighting which the train of his story seems to force

[11] Kindliness.

upon him, and apparently rejects those exhibitions which would be more affecting for the sake of those which are more easy.

It may be observed that in many of his plays the latter part is evidently neglected. When he found himself near the end of his work and in view of his reward, he shortened the labor to snatch the profit. He therefore remits his efforts where he should most vigorously exert them, and his catastrophe is improbably produced or imperfectly represented.

He had no regard to distinction of time or place but gives to one age or nation without scruple the customs, institutions, and opinions of another at the expense not only of likelihood but of possibility. These faults Pope has endeavored, with more zeal than judgment, to transfer to his imagined interpolators. We need not wonder to find Hector quoting Aristotle when we see the loves of Theseus and Hippolyta combined with the Gothic mythology of fairies. Shakespeare, indeed, was not the only violator of chronology, for in the same age Sidney, who wanted not the advantages of learning, has in his *Arcadia* confounded the pastoral with the feudal times, the days of innocence, quiet, and security with those of turbulence, violence, and adventure.

In his comic scenes he is seldom very successful when he engages his characters in reciprocations of smartness and contests of sarcasm; their jests are commonly gross and their pleasantry licentious; neither his gentlemen nor his ladies have much delicacy nor are sufficiently distinguished from his clowns by any appearance of refined manners. Whether he represented the real conversation of his time is not easy to determine; the reign of Elizabeth is commonly supposed to have been a time of stateliness, formality, and reserve, yet perhaps the relaxations of that severity were not very elegant. There must, however, have been always some modes of gaiety preferable to others, and a writer ought to choose the best.

In tragedy his performance seems constantly to be worse as his labor is more. The effusions of passion which exigence forces out are for the most part striking and energetic; but whenever he solicits his invention or strains his faculties, the offspring of his throes is tumor, meanness, tediousness, and obscurity.

In narration he affects a disproportionate pomp of diction and a wearisome train of circumlocution and tells the incident imperfectly in many words which might have been more plainly delivered in few.

Narration in dramatic poetry is naturally tedious as it is unanimated and inactive and obstructs the progress of the action; it should therefore always be rapid and enlivened by frequent interruption. Shakespeare found it an encumbrance and instead of lightening it by brevity, endeavored to recommend it by dignity and splendor.

His declamations or set speeches are commonly cold and weak, for his power was the power of nature; when he endeavored, like other tragic writers, to catch opportunities, and instead of inquiring what the occasion demanded, to show how much his stores of knowledge could supply, he seldom escapes without the pity or resentment of his reader.

It is incident to him to be now and then entangled with an unwieldy sentiment, which he cannot well express and will not reject; he struggles with it a while, and if it continues stubborn, comprises it in words such as occur and leaves it to be disentangled and evolved by those who have more leisure to bestow upon it.

Not that always where the language is intricate the thought is subtle, or the image always great where the line is bulky; the equality of words to things is very often neglected, and trivial sentiments and vulgar ideas disappoint the attention to which they are recommended by sonorous epithets and swelling figures.

But the admirers of this great poet have most reason to complain when he approaches nearest to his highest excellence and seems fully resolved to sink them in dejection and mollify them with tender emotions by the fall of greatness, the danger of innocence, or the crosses of love. What he does best he soon ceases to do. He is not long soft and pathetic without some idle conceit or contemptible equivocation. He no sooner begins to move than he counteracts himself; and terror and pity, as they are rising in the mind, are checked and blasted by sudden frigidity.

A quibble[12] is to Shakespeare what luminous vapors are to the traveler; he follows it at all adventures; it is sure to lead him out of his way and sure to engulf him in the mire. It has some malignant power over his mind, and its fascinations are irresistible. Whatever be the dignity or profundity of his disquisition, whether he be enlarging knowledge or exalting affection, whether he be amusing attention with

[12] Pun, wordplay.

incidents or enchaining it in suspense, let but a quibble spring up before him and he leaves his work unfinished. A quibble is the golden apple for which he will always turn aside from his career or stoop from his elevation. A quibble, poor and barren as it is, gave him such delight that he was content to purchase it by the sacrifice of reason, propriety, and truth. A quibble was to him the fatal Cleopatra for which he lost the world and was content to lose it.

It will be thought strange that in enumerating the defects of this writer, I have not yet mentioned his neglect of the unities, his violation of those laws which have been instituted and established by the joint authority of poets and of critics.

For his other deviations from the art of writing I resign him to critical justice without making any other demand in his favor than that which must be indulged to all human excellence: that his virtues be rated with his failings; but from the censure which this irregularity may bring upon him, I shall, with due reverence to that learning which I must oppose, adventure to try how I can defend him.

His histories, being neither tragedies nor comedies, are not subject to any of their laws; nothing more is necessary to all the praise which they expect than that the changes of action be so prepared as to be understood, that the incidents be various and affecting, and the characters consistent, natural, and distinct. No other unity is intended, and therefore none is to be sought.

In his other works he has well enough preserved the unity of action. He has not, indeed, an intrigue regularly perplexed and regularly unravelled; he does not endeavor to hide his design only to discover it, for this is seldom the order of real events, and Shakespeare is the poet of nature; but his plan has commonly what Aristotle requires, a beginning, a middle, and an end; one event is concatenated with another, and the conclusion follows by easy consequence. There are perhaps some incidents that might be spared, as in other poets there is much talk that only fills up time upon the stage; but the general system makes gradual advances, and the end of the play is the end of the expectation.

To the unities of time and place he has shown no regard; and perhaps a nearer view of the principles on which they stand will diminish their value and withdraw from them the veneration which, from the time of Corneille, they have very generally received by discovering that they have given more trouble to the poet than pleasure to the auditor.

The necessity of observing the unities of time and place arises from the supposed necessity of making the drama credible. The critics hold it impossible that an action of months or years can be possibly believed to pass in three hours; or that the spectator can suppose himself to sit in the theater while ambassadors go and return between distant kings, while armies are levied and towns besieged, while an exile wanders and returns, or till he whom they saw courting his mistress shall lament the untimely fall of his son. The mind revolts from evident falsehood, and fiction loses its force when it departs from the resemblance of reality.

From the narrow limitation of time necessarily arises the contraction of place. The spectator, who knows that he saw the first act at Alexandria, cannot suppose that he sees the next at Rome, at a distance to which not the dragons of Medea could in so short a time have transported him; he knows with certainty that he has not changed his place, and he knows that place cannot change itself, that what was a house cannot become a plain, that what was Thebes can never be Persepolis.

Such is the triumphant language with which a critic exults over the misery of an irregular poet, and exults commonly without resistance or reply. It is time, therefore, to tell him by the authority of Shakespeare that he assumes as an unquestionable principle a position which, while his breath is forming it into words, his understanding pronounces to be false. It is false that any representation is mistaken for reality, that any dramatic fable in its materiality was ever credible or for a single moment was ever credited.

The objection arising from the impossibility of passing the first hour at Alexandria and the next at Rome supposes that when the play opens, the spectator really imagines himself at Alexandria and believes that his walk to the theater has been a voyage to Egypt and that he lives in the days of Antony and Cleopatra. Surely he that imagines this may imagine more. He that can take the stage at one time for the palace of the Ptolemies may take it in half an hour for the promontory of Actium. Delusion, if delusion be admitted, has no certain limitation; if the spectator can be once persuaded that his old acquaintance are Alexander and Caesar, that a room illuminated with candles is the plain of Pharsalia or the bank of Granicus, he is in a state of elevation above the reach of reason or of truth and from the heights of empyrean poetry may despise the circumscriptions of terrestrial nature. There is no reason why a mind thus wandering in ecstasy should count the clock, or why an hour should not be a century in that calenture[13] of the brain that can make the stage a field.

The truth is that the spectators are always in their senses and know, from the first act to the last, that the stage is only a stage and that the players are only players. They come to hear a certain number of lines recited with just gesture and elegant modulation. The lines relate to some action, and an action must be in some place; but the different actions that complete a story may be in places very remote from each other; and where is the absurdity of allowing that space to represent first Athens and then Sicily which was always known to be neither Sicily nor Athens but a modern theater?

By supposition, as place is introduced, time may be extended; the time required by the fable elapses for the most part between the acts, for of so much of the action as is represented, the real and poetical duration is the same. If in the first act preparations for war against Mithridates are represented to be made in Rome, the event of the war may without absurdity be represented in the catastrophe as happening in Pontus; we know that there is neither war nor preparation for war; we know that we are neither in Rome nor Pontus, that neither Mithridates nor Lucullus are before us. The drama exhibits successive imitations of successive actions, and why may not the second imitation represent an action that happened years after the first if it be so connected with it that nothing but time can be supposed to intervene? Time is of all modes of existence most obsequious to the imagination; a lapse of years is as easily conceived as a passage of hours. In contemplation we easily contract the time of real actions and therefore willingly permit it to be contracted when we only see their imitation.

It will be asked how the drama moves if it is not credited. It is credited with all the credit due to a drama. It is credited, whenever it moves, as a just picture of a real original, as representing to the auditor what he would himself feel if he were to do or suffer what is there feigned to be suffered or to be done. The reflection that strikes the

---

[13] Delirium.

heart is not that the evils before us are real evils but that they are evils to which we ourselves may be exposed. If there be any fallacy, it is not that we fancy the players but that we fancy ourselves unhappy for a moment; but we rather lament the possibility than suppose the presence of misery, as a mother weeps over her babe when she remembers that death may take it from her. The delight of tragedy proceeds from our consciousness of fiction; if we thought murders and treasons real, they would please no more.

Imitations produce pain or pleasure not because they are mistaken for realities but because they bring realities to mind. When the imagination is recreated by a painted landscape, the trees are not supposed capable to give us shade or the fountains coolness, but we consider how we should be pleased with such fountains playing beside us and such woods waving over us. We are agitated in reading the history of *Henry the Fifth,* yet no man takes his book for the field of Agincourt. A dramatic exhibition is a book recited with concomitants that increase or diminish its effect. Familiar comedy is often more powerful in the theater than on the page; imperial tragedy is always less. The humor of Petruchio may be heightened by grimace, but what voice or what gesture can hope to add dignity or force to the soliloquy of Cato?

A play read affects the mind like a play acted. It is therefore evident that the action is not supposed to be real, and it follows that between the acts a longer or shorter time may be allowed to pass and that no more account of space or duration is to be taken by the auditor of a drama than by the reader of a narrative, before whom may pass in an hour the life of a hero or the revolutions of an empire.

Whether Shakespeare knew the unities and rejected them by design, or deviated from them by happy ignorance, it is, I think, impossible to decide and useless to enquire. We may reasonably suppose that when he rose to notice, he did not want the counsels and admonitions of scholars and critics, and that he at last deliberately persisted in a practice which he might have begun by chance. As nothing is essential to the fable but unity of action, and as the unities of time and place arise evidently from false assumptions and, by circumscribing the extent of the drama, lessen its variety, I cannot think it much to be lamented that they were not known by him or not observed; nor, if such another poet could arise, should I very vehemently reproach him that his first act passed at Venice and his next in Cyprus. Such violations of rules merely positive become[14] the comprehensive genius of Shakespeare, and such censures are suitable to the minute and slender criticism of Voltaire:

Non usque adeo permiscuit imis
Longus summa dies, ut non, si voce Metelli
Serventur leges, malint a Caesare tolli.[15]

Yet when I speak thus slightly of dramatic rules, I cannot but recollect how much wit and learning may be produced against me; before such authorities I am afraid to stand, not that I think the present question one of those that are to be decided by mere authority but because it is to be suspected that these precepts have not been so easily received but for better reasons than I have yet been able to find. The result of my enquiries, in which it would be ludicrous to boast of impartiality, is that the unities of time and place are not essential to a just drama, that though they may sometimes conduce to pleasure, they are always to be sacrificed to the nobler beauties of variety and instruction, and that a play written with nice observation of critical rules is to be contemplated as an elaborate curiosity, as the product of superfluous and ostentatious art by which is shown rather what is possible than what is necessary.

He that without diminution of any other excellence shall preserve all the unities unbroken deserves the like applause with the architect who shall display all the orders of architecture in a citadel without any deduction from its strength; but the principal beauty of a citadel is to exclude the enemy, and the greatest graces of a play are to copy nature and instruct life.

Perhaps what I have here not dogmatically but deliberately written may recall the principles of the drama to a new examination. I am almost frighted at my own temerity, and when I estimate the fame and the strength of those that maintain the contrary opinion, am ready to

---

[14] Positive: arbitrary; become: suit; i.e. such violations of merely arbitrary rules are appropriate for Shakespeare's genius.

[15] Lucan's *Pharsalia,* III, 138 ff.: "They would rather have the laws broken by Caesar than upheld by Metellus"; i.e. rather broken by a greater man than upheld by a lesser one.

sink down in reverential silence, as Aeneas withdrew from the defence of Troy when he saw Neptune shaking the wall and Juno heading the besiegers.

Those whom my arguments cannot persuade to give their approbation to the judgment of Shakespeare will easily, if they consider the condition of his life, make some allowance for his ignorance.

Every man's performance, to be rightly estimated, must be compared with the state of the age in which he lived and with his own particular opportunities; and though to the reader a book be not worse or better for the circumstances of the author, yet as there is always a silent reference of human works to human abilities, and as the enquiry how far man may extend his designs or how high he may rate his native force is of far greater dignity than in what rank we shall place any particular performance, curiosity is always busy to discover the instruments as well as to survey the workmanship to know how much is to be ascribed to original powers and how much to casual and adventitious help. The palaces of Peru or Mexico were certainly mean and incommodious habitations if compared to the houses of European monarchs, yet who could forbear to view them with astonishment who remembered that they were built without the use of iron?

The English nation in the time of Shakespeare was yet struggling to emerge from barbarity. The philology of Italy had been transplanted hither in the reign of Henry the Eighth; and the learned languages had been successfully cultivated by Lilly, Linacre, and More; by Pole, Cheke, and Gardiner; and afterwards by Smith, Clerk, Haddon, and Ascham. Greek was now taught to boys in the principal schools, and those who united elegance with learning read with great diligence the Italian and Spanish poets. But literature was yet confined to professed scholars or to men and women of high rank. The public was gross and dark, and to be able to read and write was an accomplishment still valued for its rarity.

Nations, like individuals, have their infancy. A people newly awakened to literary curiosity, being yet unacquainted with the true state of things, knows not how to judge of that which is proposed as its resemblance. Whatever is remote from common appearances is always welcome to vulgar as to childish credulity; and of a country unenlightened by learning, the whole people is vulgar. The study of those who then aspired to plebeian learning was laid out upon adventures, giants, dragons, and enchantments. *The Death of Arthur* was the favorite volume.

The mind which has feasted on the luxurious wonders of fiction has no taste for the insipidity of truth. A play which imitated only the common occurrences of the world would upon the admirers of *Palmerin* and *Guy of Warwick* have made little impression; he that wrote for such an audience was under the necessity of looking round for strange events and fabulous transactions, and that incredibility by which maturer knowledge is offended was the chief recommendation of writings to unskillful curiosity.

Our author's plots are generally borrowed from novels, and it is reasonable to suppose that he chose the most popular, such as were read by many and related by more, for his audience could not have followed him through the intricacies of the drama had they not held the thread of the story in their hands.

The stories which we now find only in remoter authors were in his time accessible and familiar. The fable of *As You Like It,* which is supposed to be copied from Chaucer's *Gamelyn,* was a little pamphlet of those times, and old Mr. Cibber remembered the tale of *Hamlet* in plain English prose which the critics have now to seek in Saxo Grammaticus.

His English histories he took from English chronicles and English ballads; and as the ancient writers were made known to his countrymen by versions,[16] they supplied him with new subjects; he dilated some of Plutarch's lives into plays when they had been translated by North.

His plots, whether historical or fabulous, are always crowded with incidents by which the attention of a rude people was more easily caught than by sentiment or argumentation, and such is the power of the marvelous even over those who despise it that every man finds his mind more strongly seized by the tragedies of Shakespeare than of any other writer; others please us by particular speeches, but he always makes us anxious for the event and has perhaps excelled all but Homer in securing the first purpose of a writer by exciting restless and unquenchable curiosity and compelling him that reads his work to read it through.

---

[16] Translations.

The shows and bustle with which his plays abound have the same original. As knowledge advances, pleasure passes from the eye to the ear, but returns as it declines from the ear to the eye. Those to whom our author's labors were exhibited had more skill in pomps or processions than in poetical language and perhaps wanted some visible and discriminated events as comments on the dialogue. He knew how he should most please; and whether his practice is more agreeable to nature or whether his example has prejudiced the nation, we still find that on our stage something must be done as well as said, and inactive declamation is very coldly heard, however musical or elegant, passionate or sublime.

Voltaire expresses his wonder that our author's extravagances are endured by a nation which has seen the tragedy of *Cato*. Let him be answered that Addison speaks the language of poets, and Shakespeare, of men. We find in *Cato* innumerable beauties which enamor us of its author, but we see nothing that acquaints us with human sentiments or human actions; we place it with the fairest and the noblest progeny which judgment propagates by conjunction with learning; but *Othello* is the vigorous and vivacious offspring of observation impregnated by genius. *Cato* affords a splendid exhibition of artificial and fictitious manners and delivers just and noble sentiments in diction easy, elevated, and harmonious, but its hopes and fear communicate no vibration to the heart; the composition refers us only to the writer; we pronounce the name of *Cato,* but we think on Addison.

The work of a correct and regular writer is a garden accurately formed and diligently planted, varied with shades and scented with flowers; the composition of Shakespeare is a forest in which oaks extend their branches and pines tower in the air, interspersed sometimes with weeds and brambles and sometimes giving shelter to myrtles and to roses, filling the eye with awful pomp and gratifying the mind with endless diversity. Other poets display cabinets of precious rarities, minutely finished, wrought into shape and polished unto brightness. Shakespeare opens a mine which contains gold and diamonds in inexhaustible plenty, though clouded by incrustations, debased by impurities, and mingled with a mass of meaner minerals.

It has been much disputed whether Shakespeare owed his excellence to his own native force or whether he had the common helps of scholastic education, the precepts of critical science, and the examples of ancient authors.

There has always prevailed a tradition that Shakespeare wanted learning, that he had no regular education nor much skill in the dead languages. Jonson, his friend, affirms that "he had small Latin, and no Greek," who, besides that he had no imaginable temptation to falsehood, wrote at a time when the character and acquisitions of Shakespeare were known to multitudes. His evidence ought therefore to decide the controversy unless some testimony of equal force could be opposed.

Some have imagined that they have discovered deep learning in many imitations of old writers; but the examples which I have known urged were drawn from books translated in his time, or were such easy coincidences of thought as will happen to all who consider the same subjects, or such remarks on life or axioms of morality as float in conversation and are transmitted through the world in proverbial sentences.

I have found it remarked that in this important sentence, "Go before, I'll follow," we read a translation of *I prae, sequar.* I have been told that when Caliban after a pleasing dream says, "I cry'd to sleep again," the author imitates Anacreon, who had, like every other man, the same wish on the same occasion.[17]

There are a few passages which may pass for imitations, but so few that the exception only confirms the rule; he obtained them from accidental quotations or by oral communication, and as he used what he had, would have used more if he had obtained it.

The *Comedy of Errors* is confessedly taken from the *Menaechmi* of Plautus, from the only play of Plautus which was then in English. What can be more probable than that he who copied that would have copied more, but that those which were not translated were inaccessible?

Whether he knew the modern languages is uncertain. That his plays have some French scenes proves but little; he might easily procure them to be written, and probably, even though he had known

---

[17] In "The Dream," an ode attributed to the Greek poet Anacreon, the speaker, awakening from a delightful dream, wishes to sleep again.

the language in the common degree, he could not have written it without assistance. In the story of *Romeo and Juliet* he is observed to have followed the English translation where it deviates from the Italian, but this on the other part proves nothing against his knowledge of the original. He was to copy not what he knew himself, but what was known to his audience.

It is most likely that he had learned Latin sufficiently to make him acquainted with construction but that he never advanced to an easy perusal of the Roman authors. Concerning his skill in modern languages I can find no sufficient ground of determination; but as no imitations of French or Italian authors have been discovered, though the Italian poetry was then high in esteem, I am inclined to believe that he read little more than English and chose for his fables only such tales as he found translated.

That much knowledge is scattered over his works is very justly observed by Pope, but it is often such knowledge as books did not supply. He that will understand Shakespeare must not be content to study him in the closet;[18] he must look for his meaning sometimes among the sports of the field and sometimes among the manufactures of the shop.

There is, however, proof enough that he was a very diligent reader, nor was our language then so indigent of books but that he might very liberally indulge his curiosity without excursion into foreign literature. Many of the Roman authors were translated and some of the Greek; the Reformation had filled the kingdom with theological learning; most of the topics of human disquisition had found English writers; and poetry had been cultivated not only with diligence but success. This was a stock of knowledge sufficient for a mind so capable of appropriating and improving it.

But the greater part of his excellence was the product of his own genius. He found the English stage in a state of the utmost rudeness; no essays either in tragedy or comedy had appeared from which it could be discovered to what degree of delight either one or other might be carried. Neither character nor dialogue were yet understood. Shakespeare may be truly said to have introduced them both amongst us and in some of his happier scenes to have carried them both to the utmost height.

---

[18] Small private room or study.

By what gradations of improvement he proceeded is not easily known, for the chronology of his works is yet unsettled. Rowe is of opinion that "perhaps we are not to look for his beginning, like those of other writers, in his least perfect works; art had so little, and nature so large a share in what he did, that for ought I know," says he, "the performances of his youth, as they were the most vigorous, were the best." But the power of nature is only the power of using to any certain purpose the materials which diligence procures or opportunity supplies. Nature gives no man knowledge and, when images are collected by study and experience, can only assist in combining or applying them. Shakespeare, however favored by nature, could impart only what he had learned; and as he must increase his ideas, like other mortals, by gradual acquisition, he, like them, grew wiser as he grew older, could display life better as he knew it more, and instruct with more efficacy as he was himself more amply instructed.

There is a vigilance of observation and accuracy of distinction which books and precepts cannot confer; from this almost all original and native excellence proceeds. Shakespeare must have looked upon mankind with perspicacity in the highest degree curious and attentive. Other writers borrow their characters from preceding writers and diversify them only by the accidental appendages of present manners; the dress is a little varied, but the body is the same. Our author had both matter and form to provide; for except the characters of Chaucer, to whom I think he is not much indebted, there were no writers in English and perhaps not many in other modern languages which showed life in its native colors.

The contest about the original benevolence or malignity of man had not yet commenced. Speculation had not yet attempted to analyze the mind, to trace the passions to their sources, to unfold the seminal principles of vice and virtue, or sound the depths of the heart for the motives of action. All those enquiries, which from that time that human nature became the fashionable study have been made sometimes with nice discernment but often with idle subtlety, were yet unattempted. The tales with which the infancy of learning was satisfied exhibited only the superficial appearances of action, related the events but omitted the causes, and were formed for such as delighted in the wonders rather than in truth. Mankind was not then to be studied in the closet; he that would know the world was under the necessity of gleaning his own remarks by mingling as he could in its business and amusements.

Boyle congratulated himself upon his high birth because it favored his curiosity by facilitating his access. Shakespeare had no such advantage; he came to London a needy adventurer and lived for a time by very mean employments. Many works of genius and learning have been performed in states of life that appear very little favorable to thought or to enquiry; so many that he who considers them is inclined to think that he sees enterprise and perseverance predominating over all external agency and bidding help and hindrance vanish before them. The genius of Shakespeare was not to be depressed by the weight of poverty nor limited by the narrow conversation to which men in want are inevitably condemned; the encumbrances of his fortune were shaken from his mind "as dewdrops from a lion's mane."

Though he had so many little difficulties to encounter and so little assistance to surmount them, he has been able to obtain an exact knowledge of many modes of life and many casts of native dispositions, to vary them with great multiplicity, to mark them by nice distinctions, and to show them in full view by proper combinations. In this part of his performances he had none to imitate but has himself been imitated by all succeeding writers, and it may be doubted whether from all his successors more maxims of theoretical knowledge or more rules of practical prudence can be collected than he alone has given to his country.

Nor was his attention confined to the actions of men; he was an exact surveyor of the inanimate world; his descriptions have always some peculiarities gathered by contemplating things as they really exist. It may be observed that the oldest poets of many nations preserve their reputation and that the following generations of wit, after a short celebrity, sink into oblivion. The first, whoever they be, must take their sentiments and descriptions immediately from knowledge; the resemblance is therefore just, their descriptions are verified by every eye and their sentiments acknowledged by every breast. Those whom their fame invites to the same studies copy partly them and partly nature, till the books of one age gain such authority as to stand in the place of nature to another, and imitation, always deviating a little, becomes at last capricious and casual. Shakespeare, whether life or nature be his subject, shows plainly that he has seen with his own eyes; he gives the image which he receives, not weakened or distorted by the intervention of any other mind; the ignorant feel his representations to be just, and the learned see that they are complete.

Perhaps it would not be easy to find any author, except Homer, who invented so much as Shakespeare, who so much advanced the studies which he cultivated or effused so much novelty upon his age or country. The form, the characters, the language, and the shows of the English drama are his. "He seems," says Dennis, "to have been the very original of our English tragical harmony, that is, the harmony of blank verse, diversified often by dissyllable and trissyllable terminations. For the diversity distinguishes it from heroic harmony, and by bringing it nearer to common use makes it more proper to gain attention, and more fit for action and dialogue. Such verse we make when we are writing prose; we make such verse in common conversation."

I know not whether this praise is rigorously just. The dissyllable termination, which the critic rightly appropriates to the drama, is to be found, though, I think, not in *Gorboduc,* which is confessedly before our author, yet in *Hieronimo,*[19] of which the date is not certain but which there is reason to believe at least as old as his earliest plays. This, however, is certain, that he is the first who taught either tragedy or comedy to please, there being no theatrical piece of any older writer of which the name is known except to antiquaries and collectors of books which are sought because they are scarce, and would not have been scarce, had they been much esteemed.

To him we must ascribe the praise, unless Spenser may divide it with him, of having first discovered to how much smoothness and harmony the English language could be softened. He has speeches, perhaps sometimes scenes, which have all the delicacy of Rowe without his effeminacy. He endeavors indeed commonly to strike by the force and vigor of his dialogue, but he never executes his purpose better than when he tries to soothe by softness.

Yet it must be at last confessed that as we owe everything to him, he owes something to us; that if much of his praise is paid by percep-

---

[19] Thomas Kyd's *Spanish Tragedy* (1592).

tion and judgment, much is likewise given by custom and veneration. We fix our eyes upon his graces and turn them from his deformities, and endure in him what we should in another loathe or despise. If we endured without praising, respect for the father of our drama might excuse us; but I have seen in the book of some modern critic a collection of anomalies which show that he has corrupted language by every mode of depravation but which his admirer has accumulated as a monument of honor.

He has scenes of undoubted and perpetual excellence but perhaps not one play which, if it were now exhibited as the work of a contemporary writer, would be heard to the conclusion. I am indeed far from thinking that his works were wrought to his own ideas of perfection; when they were such as would satisfy the audience, they satisfied the writer. It is seldom that authors, though more studious of fame than Shakespeare, rise much above the standard of their own age; to add a little of what is best will always be sufficient for present praise, and those who find themselves exalted into fame are willing to credit their encomiasts and to spare the labor of contending with themselves.

It does not appear that Shakespeare thought his works worthy of posterity, that he levied any ideal tribute upon future times or had any further prospect than of present popularity and present profit. When his plays had been acted, his hope was at an end; he solicited no addition of honor from the reader. He therefore made no scruple to repeat the same jests in many dialogues or to entangle different plots by the same knot of perplexity, which may be at least forgiven him by those who recollect that of Congreve's four comedies, two are concluded by a marriage in a mask, by a deception which perhaps never happened and which, whether likely or not, he did not invent.

So careless was this great poet of future fame that, though he retired to ease and plenty while he was yet little "declined into the vale of years," before he could be disgusted with fatigue or disabled by infirmity, he made no collection of his works nor desired to rescue those that had been already published from the depravations that obscured them or secure to the rest a better destiny by giving them to the world in their genuine state. . . .

(The remainder of the Preface deals with earlier editions of Shakespeare and Johnson's own editorial policies.)

NOTES ON THE PLAYS OF WILLIAM SHAKESPEARE

On KING HENRY IV, Part Two

. . . None of Shakespeare's plays are more read than the *First and Second Parts of Henry the Fourth.* Perhaps no author has ever in two plays afforded so much delight. The great events are interesting, for the fate of kingdoms depends upon them; the slighter occurrences are diverting and, except one or two, sufficiently probable; the incidents are multiplied with wonderful fertility of invention and the characters diversified with the utmost nicety of discernment and the profoundest skill in the nature of man.

The prince, who is the hero both of the comic and tragic part, is a young man of great abilities and violent passions, whose sentiments are right though his actions are wrong, whose virtues are obscured by negligence and whose understanding is dissipated by levity. In his idle hours he is rather loose than wicked, and when the occasion forces out his latent qualities, he is great without effort and brave without tumult. The trifler is roused into a hero, and the hero again reposes in the trifler. This character is great, original, and just. . . .

But Falstaff, unimitated, unimitable Falstaff, how shall I describe thee? Thou compound of sense and vice: of sense which may be admired but not esteemed, of vice which may be despised but hardly detested. Falstaff is a character loaded with faults, and with those faults which naturally produce contempt. He is a thief and a glutton, a coward and a boaster, always ready to cheat the weak and prey upon the poor, to terrify the timorous and insult the defenseless. At once obsequious and malignant, he satirizes in their absence those whom he lives by flattering. He is familiar with the prince only as an agent of vice, but of this familiarity he is so proud as not only to be supercilious and haughty with common men but to think his interest of importance to the Duke of Lancaster. Yet the man thus corrupt, thus despicable, makes himself necessary to the prince that despises him by the most pleasing of all qualities, perpetual gaiety, by an unfailing power of exciting laughter, which is the more freely indulged as his wit is not of the splendid or ambitious kind but consists in easy escapes and sallies of levity which make sport but raise no envy. It must be observed that he is stained with no enormous or sanguinary crimes, so that his licentiousness is not so offensive but that it may be borne for his mirth.

The moral to be drawn from this representation is that no man is more dangerous than he that with a will to corrupt hath the power to please, and that neither wit nor honesty ought to think themselves safe with such a companion when they see Henry seduced by Falstaff.

Concluding note[20]

On KING LEAR

The tragedy of *Lear* is deservedly celebrated among the dramas of Shakespeare. There is perhaps no play which keeps the attention so strongly fixed, which so much agitates our passions and interests our curiosity. The artful involutions of distinct interests, the striking opposition of contrary characters, the sudden changes of fortune, and the quick succession of events fill the mind with a perpetual tumult of indignation, pity, and hope. There is no scene which does not contribute to the aggravation of the distress or conduct of the action, and scarce a line which does not conduce to the progress of the scene. So powerful is the current of the poet's imagination that the mind which once ventures within it is hurried irresistibly along.

On the seeming improbability of Lear's conduct it may be observed that he is represented according to the histories at that time vulgarly[21] received as true. And perhaps if we turn our thoughts upon the barbarity and ignorance of the age to which this story is referred, it will appear not so unlikely as while we estimate Lear's manners by our own. Such preference of one daughter to another or resignation of dominion on such conditions would be yet credible if told of a petty prince of Guinea or Madagascar. Shakespeare, indeed, by the mention of his earls and dukes has given us the idea of times more civilized and of life regulated by softer manners; and the truth is that though he so

---

[20] In his edition, Johnson not only provided explanatory footnotes to clarify specific passages but also gave a brief general commentary on each play in his concluding note.

[21] Commonly, by ordinary people.

nicely discriminates and so minutely describes the characters of men, he commonly neglects and confounds the characters of ages by mingling customs ancient and modern, English and foreign.

My learned friend Mr. Warton, who has in the *Adventurer* very minutely criticized this play, remarks that the instances of cruelty are too savage and shocking, and that the intervention of Edmund destroys the simplicity of the story. These objections may, I think, be answered by repeating that the cruelty of the daughters is an historical fact to which the poet has added little, having only drawn it into a series by dialogue and action. But I am not able to apologize with equal plausibility for the extrusion[22] of Gloucester's eyes, which seems an act too horrid to be endured in dramatic exhibition and such as must always compel the mind to relieve its distress by incredulity. Yet let it be remembered that our author well knew what would please the audience for which he wrote.

The injury done by Edmund to the simplicity of the action is abundantly recompensed by the addition of variety, by the art with which he is made to co-operate with the chief design and the opportunity which he gives the poet of combining perfidy with perfidy and connecting the wicked son with the wicked daughters, to impress this important moral, that villainy is never at a stop, that crimes lead to crimes and at last terminate in ruin.

But though this moral be incidentally enforced, Shakespeare has suffered the virtue of Cordelia to perish in a just cause contrary to the natural ideas of justice, to the hope of the reader, and, what is yet more strange, to the faith of chronicles. Yet this conduct is justified by the Spectator, who blames Tate for giving Cordelia success and happiness in his alteration[23] and declares that, in his opinion, "the tragedy has lost half its beauty." Dennis has remarked, whether justly or not, that to secure the favorable reception of *Cato,* "the town was poisoned with much false and abominable criticism," and that endeavors had been used to discredit and decry poetical justice. A play in which the wicked prosper and the virtuous miscarry may doubtless be good

---

[22] Thrusting or plucking out; i.e. his blinding.

[23] In Nahum Tate's revision, which was popular in the eighteenth century, Cordelia is saved and marries Edgar. The *Spectator* essay, No. 40, was written by Joseph Addison.

because it is a just representation of the common events of human life; but since all reasonable beings naturally love justice, I cannot easily be persuaded that the observation of justice makes a play worse, or that, if other excellencies are equal, the audience will not always rise better pleased from the final triumph of persecuted virtue.

In the present case the public has decided. Cordelia, from the time of Tate, has always retired with victory and felicity. And if my sensations could add anything to the general suffrage, I might relate I was many years ago so shocked by Cordelia's death that I know not whether I ever endured to read again the last scenes of the play till I undertook to revise them as an editor.

There is another controversy among the critics concerning this play. It is disputed whether the predominant image in Lear's disordered mind be the loss of his kingdom or the cruelty of his daughters. Mr. Murphy, a very judicious critic, has evinced by induction of particular passages that the cruelty of his daughters is the primary source of his distress and that the loss of royalty affects him only as a secondary and subordinate evil. He observes with great justness that Lear would move our compassion but little did we not rather consider the injured father than the degraded king.

Concluding note

On HAMLET

This account[24] of the character of Polonius, though it sufficiently reconciles the seeming inconsistency of so much wisdom with so much folly, does not perhaps correspond exactly to the ideas of our author. The commentator makes the character of Polonius a character only of manners, discriminated by properties superficial, accidental, and acquired. The poet intended a nobler delineation of a mixed character of manners and of nature.[25] Polonius is a man bred in courts,

[24] Johnson is taking issue with the critic William Warburton's interpretation of the character of Polonius.

[25] By "character of manners" Johnson meant social types, subject to changes as the times change; by "character of nature," more universal psychological or moral types that remain constant.

exercised in business, stored with observations, confident of his knowledge, proud of his eloquence, and declining into dotage. His mode of oratory is truly represented as designed to ridicule the practice of those times, of prefaces that made no introduction and of method that embarrassed rather than explained. This part of his character is accidental, the rest is natural. Such a man is positive and confident because he knows that his mind was once strong and knows not that it is become weak. Such a man excels in general principles but fails in the particular application. He is knowing in retrospect and ignorant in foresight. While he depends upon his memory and can draw from his repositories of knowledge, he utters weighty sentences and gives useful counsel; but as the mind in its enfeebled state cannot be kept long busy and intent, the old man is subject to sudden dereliction of his faculties, he loses the order of his ideas and entangles himself in his own thoughts till he recovers the leading principle and falls again into his former train. This idea of dotage encroaching upon wisdom will solve all the phenomena of the character of Polonius.

Note on II, ii, 86 ff.

If the dramas of Shakespeare were to be characterized each by the particular excellence which distinguishes it from the rest, we must allow to the tragedy of *Hamlet* the praise of variety. The incidents are so numerous that the argument of the play would make a long tale. The scenes are interchangeably diversified with merriment and solemnity: with merriment that includes judicious and instructive observations, and solemnity not strained by poetical violence above the natural sentiments of man. New characters appear from time to time in continual succession, exhibiting various forms of life and particular modes of conversation. The pretended madness of Hamlet causes much mirth, the mournful distraction of Ophelia fills the heart with tenderness, and every personage produces the effect intended, from the apparition that in the first act chills the blood with horror to the fop in the last that exposes affectation to just contempt.

The conduct is perhaps not wholly secure against objections. The action is indeed for the most part in continual progression, but there are some scenes which neither forward nor retard it. Of the feigned madness of Hamlet there appears no adequate cause, for he does nothing which he might not have done with the reputation of sanity. He plays the madman most when he treats Ophelia with so much rudeness, which seems to be useless and wanton cruelty.

Hamlet is through the whole play rather an instrument than an agent. After he has by the stratagem of the play convicted the king, he makes no attempt to punish him, and his death is at last effected by an incident which Hamlet has no part in producing.

The catastrophe is not very happily produced; the exchange of weapons is rather an expedient of necessity than a stroke of art. A scheme might easily have been formed to kill Hamlet with the dagger and Laertes with the bowl.

The poet is accused of having shown little regard to poetical justice and may be charged with equal neglect of poetical probability. The apparition left the regions of the dead to little purpose; the revenge which he demands is not obtained but by the death of him that was required to take it; and the gratification which would arise from the destruction of an usurper and a murderer is abated by the untimely death of Ophelia, the young, the beautiful, the harmless, and the pious.

Concluding note

On OTHELLO

The beauties of this play impress themselves so strongly upon the attention of the reader that they can draw no aid from critical illustration. The fiery openness of Othello, magnanimous, artless, and credulous, boundless in his confidence, ardent in his affection, inflexible in his resolution, and obdurate in his revenge; the cool malignity of Iago, silent in his resentment, subtle in his designs, and studious at once of his interest and his vengeance; the soft simplicity of Desdemona, confident of merit and conscious of innocence, her artless perseverance in her suit and her slowness to suspect that she can be suspected, are such proofs of Shakespeare's skill in human nature as, I suppose, it is vain to seek in any modern writer. The gradual progress which Iago makes in the Moor's conviction and the circumstances which he employs to enflame him are so artfully natural that though it will perhaps not be said of him, as he says of himself, that he is "a man not easily jealous," yet we cannot but pity him when at last we find him "perplexed in the extreme."

There is always danger lest wickedness conjoined with abilities should steal upon esteem though it misses of approbation, but the character of Iago is so conducted that he is from the first scene to the last hated and despised.

Even the inferior characters of this play would be very conspicuous in any other piece, not only for their justness but their strength. Cassio is brave, benevolent, and honest, ruined only by his want of stubbornness to resist an insidious invitation. Roderigo's suspicious credulity and impatient submission to the cheats which he sees practiced upon him, and which by persuasion he suffers to be repeated, exhibit a strong picture of a weak mind betrayed by unlawful desires to a false friend; and the virtue of Emilia is such as we often find, worn loosely but not cast off, easy to commit small crimes but quickened and alarmed at atrocious villainies.

The scenes from the beginning to the end are busy, varied by happy interchanges, and regularly presenting the progression of the story; and the narrative in the end, though it tells but what is known already, yet is necessary to produce the death of Othello.

Had the scene opened in Cyprus, and the preceding incidents been occasionally related, there had been little wanting to a drama of the most exact and scrupulous regularity.

Concluding note

4

LIVES OF THE POETS (1779–1781)

COWLEY

Cowley, like other poets who have written with narrow views and, instead of tracing intellectual pleasure to its natural sources in the mind of man, paid their court to temporary prejudices, has been at one time too much praised and too much neglected at another.

Wit, like all other things subject by their nature to the choice of man, has its changes and fashions, and at different times takes different forms. About the beginning of the seventeenth century appeared a race of writers that may be termed the metaphysical poets, of whom, in a criticism on the works of Cowley, it is not improper to give some account.[1]

The metaphysical poets were men of learning, and to show their learning was their whole endeavor; but unluckily resolving to show it in rhyme, instead of writing poetry they only wrote verses, and very often such verses as stood the trial of the finger better than of the ear, for the modulation was so imperfect that they were only found to be verses by counting the syllables.

If the father of criticism has rightly denominated poetry *τέχνη μιμητική, an imitative art,* these writers will, without great

[1] This general discussion of the metaphysical poets follows the biographical sketch of Cowley and precedes the evaluation of Cowley's poems.

wrong, lose their right to the name of poets, for they cannot be said to have imitated anything; they neither copied nature nor life, neither painted the forms of matter nor represented the operations of intellect.

Those, however, who deny them to be poets allow them to be wits. Dryden confesses of himself and his contemporaries that they fall below Donne in wit but maintains that they surpass him in poetry.

If wit be well described by Pope as being "that which has been often thought, but was never before so well expressed," they certainly never attained nor ever sought it; for they endeavored to be singular[2] in their thoughts and were careless of their diction. But Pope's account of wit is undoubtedly erroneous: he depresses it below its natural dignity and reduces it from strength of thought to happiness of language.

If by a more noble and more adequate conception that be considered as wit which is at once natural and new, that which, though not obvious, is upon its first production acknowledged to be just; if it be that which he that never found it wonders how he missed; to wit of this kind the metaphysical poets have seldom risen. Their thoughts are often new but seldom natural; they are not obvious, but neither are they just; and the reader, far from wondering that he missed them, wonders more frequently by what perverseness of industry they were ever found.

But wit, abstracted from its effects upon the hearer, may be more rigorously and philosophically considered as a kind of *discordia concors,* a combination of dissimilar images or discovery of occult resemblances in things apparently unlike. Of wit thus defined they have more than enough. The most heterogeneous ideas are yoked by violence together; nature and art are ransacked for illustrations, comparisons, and allusions; their learning instructs and their subtlety surprises; but the reader commonly thinks his improvement dearly bought and though he sometimes admires, is seldom pleased.

From this account of their compositions it will be readily inferred that they were not successful in representing or moving the affections. As they were wholly employed on something unexpected and surprising, they had no regard to that uniformity of sentiment which enables us to conceive and to excite the pains and the pleasure of other minds;

---

[2] Peculiar, strange, unique.

they never enquired what, on any occasion, they should have said or done but wrote rather as beholders than partakers of human nature; as beings looking upon good and evil, impassive and at leisure; as Epicurean deities making remarks on the actions of men and the vicissitudes of life without interest and without emotion. Their courtship was void of fondness and their lamentation of sorrow. Their wish was only to say what they hoped had been never said before.

Nor was the sublime more within their reach than the pathetic, for they never attempted that comprehension and expanse of thought which at once fills the whole mind and of which the first effect is sudden astonishment and the second rational admiration. Sublimity is produced by aggregation and littleness by dispersion. Great thoughts are always general, and consist in positions not limited by exceptions and in descriptions not descending to minuteness. It is with great propriety that subtlety, which in its original import means exility[3] of particles, is taken in its metaphorical meaning for nicety of distinction. Those writers who lay on the watch for novelty could have little hope of greatness, for great things cannot have escaped former observation. Their attempts were always analytic; they broke every image into fragments and could no more represent, by their slender conceits and labored particularities, the prospects of nature or the scenes of life than he who dissects a sun-beam with a prism can exhibit the wide effulgence of a summer noon.

What they wanted,[4] however, of the sublime, they endeavored to supply by hyperbole; their amplification had no limits; they left not only reason but fancy behind them and produced combinations of confused magnificence that not only could not be credited but could not be imagined.

Yet great labor, directed by great abilities, is never wholly lost; if they frequently threw away their wit upon false conceits, they likewise sometimes struck out unexpected truth; if their conceits were far-fetched, they were often worth the carriage. To write on their plan, it was at least necessary to read and think. No man could be born a metaphysical poet nor assume the dignity of a writer by descriptions copied from descriptions, by imitations borrowed from imitations, by

[3] Thinness, tenuousness.

[4] Lacked.

traditional imagery and hereditary similes, by readiness of rhyme and volubility of syllables.

In perusing the works of this race of authors, the mind is exercised either by recollection or inquiry; either something already learned is to be retrieved or something new is to be examined. If their greatness seldom elevates, their acuteness often surprises; if the imagination is not always gratified, at least the powers of reflection and comparison are employed; and in the mass of materials which ingenious absurdity has thrown together, genuine wit and useful knowledge may be sometimes found, buried perhaps in grossness of expression but useful to those who know their value; and such as, when they are expanded to perspicuity and polished to elegance, may give lustre to works which have more propriety though less copiousness of sentiment.

This kind of writing, which was, I believe, borrowed from Marini and his followers, had been recommended by the example of Donne, a man of very extensive and various knowledge, and by Jonson, whose manner resembled that of Donne more in the ruggedness of his lines than in the cast of his sentiments. . . .

MILTON

Those who admire the beauties of this great poet sometimes force their own judgment into false approbation of his little pieces and prevail upon themselves to think that admirable which is only singular. All that short compositions can commonly attain is neatness and elegance. Milton never learned the art of doing little things with grace; he overlooked the milder excellence of suavity and softness; he was a "lion" that had no skill "in dandling the kid."[5]

One of the poems on which much praise has been bestowed is *Lycidas*, of which the diction is harsh, the rhymes uncertain, and the numbers unpleasing. What beauty there is we must therefore seek in the sentiments and images. It is not to be considered as the effusion of

---

[5] This critical evaluation of Milton's poems follows a long biographical account and a few comments on Milton's juvenile pieces.

real passion, for passion runs not after remote allusions and obscure opinions. Passion plucks no berries from the myrtle and ivy, nor calls upon Arethuse and Mincius, nor tells of rough "satyrs" and "fauns with cloven heel."[6] Where there is leisure for fiction there is little grief.

In this poem there is no nature, for there is no truth; there is no art, for there is nothing new. Its form is that of a pastoral, easy, vulgar,[7] and therefore disgusting; whatever images it can supply are long ago exhausted, and its inherent improbability always forces dissatisfaction on the mind. When Cowley tells of Hervey that they studied together, it is easy to suppose how much he must miss the companion of his labors and the partner of his discoveries; but what image of tenderness can be excited by these lines?

We drove a field, and both together heard
What time the grey fly winds her sultry horn,
Battening our flocks with the fresh dews of night.

We know that they never drove a field, and that they had no flocks to batten; and though it be allowed that the representation may be allegorical, the true meaning is so uncertain and remote that it is never sought because it cannot be known when it is found.

Among the flocks and copses and flowers appear the heathen deities, Jove and Phoebus, Neptune and Aeolus, with a long train of mythological imagery such as a college easily supplies. Nothing can less display knowledge or less exercise invention than to tell how a shepherd has lost his companion and must now feed his flocks alone, without any judge of his skill in piping; and how one god asks another god what is become of Lycidas, and how neither god can tell. He who thus grieves will excite no sympathy; he who thus praises will confer no honor.

This poem has yet a grosser fault. With these trifling fictions are mingled the most awful[8] and sacred truths, such as ought never to be polluted with such irreverent combinations. The shepherd likewise is

---

[6] All these echoes of earlier pastorals appear in *Lycidas*.

[7] Coarsely commonplace.

[8] Awe-inspiring.

now a feeder of sheep and afterwards an ecclesiastical pastor, a superintendent of a Christian flock. Such equivocations are always unskillful, but here they are indecent and at least approach to impiety, of which, however, I believe the writer not to have been conscious.

Such is the power of reputation justly acquired that its blaze drives away the eye from nice examination. Surely no man could have fancied that he read *Lycidas* with pleasure, had he not known its author.

Of the two pieces, *L'Allegro* and *Il Penseroso,* I believe opinion is uniform; every man that reads them, reads them with pleasure. The author's design is not, what Theobald has remarked, merely to show how objects derive their colors from the mind by representing the operation of the same things upon the gay and the melancholy temper or upon the same man as he is differently disposed, but rather how, among the successive variety of appearances, every disposition of mind takes hold on those by which it may be gratified.

The *cheerful* man hears the lark in the morning; the *pensive* man hears the nightingale in the evening. The *cheerful* man sees the cock strut and hears the horn and hounds echo in the woods, then walks "not unseen" to observe the glory of the rising sun or listen to the singing milkmaid and view the labors of the plowman and the mower, then casts his eyes about him over scenes of smiling plenty and looks up to the distant tower, the residence of some fair inhabitant; thus he pursues rural gaiety through a day of labor or of play and delights himself at night with the fanciful narratives of superstitious ignorance.

The *pensive* man at one time walks "unseen" to muse at midnight and at another hears the sullen curfew. If the weather drives him home, he sits in a room lighted only by "glowing embers" or by a lonely lamp outwatches the North Star to discover the habitation of separate souls, and varies the shades of meditation by contemplating the magnificent or pathetic scenes of tragic and epic poetry. When the morning comes, a morning gloomy with rain and wind, he walks into the dark trackless woods, falls asleep by some murmuring water, and with melancholy enthusiasm expects some dream of prognostication or some music played by aerial performers.

Both Mirth and Melancholy are solitary, silent inhabitants of the breast that neither receive nor transmit communication; no mention is therefore made of a philosophical friend or a pleasant companion. Seriousness does not arise from any participation of calamity nor gaiety from the pleasures of the bottle.

The man of *cheerfulness,* having exhausted the country, tries what "towered cities" will afford and mingles with scenes of splendor, gay assemblies, and nuptial festivities; but he mingles a mere spectator as, when the learned comedies of Jonson or the wild dramas of Shakespeare are exhibited, he attends the theater.

The *pensive* man never loses himself in crowds but walks the cloister or frequents the cathedral. Milton probably had not yet forsaken the Church.

Both his characters delight in music; but he seems to think that cheerful notes would have obtained from Pluto a complete dismission of Eurydice, of whom solemn sounds only procured a conditional release.[9]

For the old age of Cheerfulness he makes no provision, but Melancholy he conducts with great dignity to the close of life.

Through these two poems the images are properly selected and nicely distinguished, but the colors of the diction seem not sufficiently discriminated. His Cheerfulness is without levity, and his Pensiveness without asperity. I know not whether the characters are kept sufficiently apart. No mirth can, indeed, be found in his melancholy, but I am afraid that I always meet some melancholy in his mirth. They are two noble efforts of imagination.

The greatest of his juvenile performances is the *Masque of Comus*, in which may very plainly be discovered the dawn or twilight of *Paradise Lost.* Milton appears to have formed very early that system of diction and mode of verse which his maturer judgment approved and from which he never endeavored nor desired to deviate.

Nor does *Comus* afford only a specimen of his language; it exhibits likewise his power of description and his vigor of sentiment, employed in the praise and defense of virtue. A work more truly poetical is rarely found; allusions, images, and descriptive epithets

---

[9] Eurydice's release from Pluto's underworld was subject to the condition that Orpheus not look back while leading her out; he did not fulfil the condition and failed to rescue her.

embellish amost every period[10] with lavish decoration. As a series of lines, therefore, it may be considered as worthy of all the admiration with which the votaries have received it.

As a drama it is deficient. The action is not probable. A masque, in those parts where supernatural intervention is admitted, must indeed be given up to all the freaks of imagination; but so far as the action is merely human it ought to be reasonable, which can hardly be said of the conduct of the two brothers, who, when their sister sinks with fatigue in a pathless wilderness, wander both away together in search of berries too far to find their way back and leave a helpless lady to all the sadness and danger of solitude. This, however, is a defect overbalanced by its convenience.

What deserves more reprehension is that the prologue spoken in the wild wood by the Attendant Spirit is addressed to the audience, a mode of communication so contrary to the nature of dramatic representation that no precedents can support it.

The discourse of the Spirit is too long, an objection that may be made to almost all the following speeches; they have not the spriteliness of a dialogue animated by reciprocal contention but seem rather declamations deliberately composed and formally repeated on a moral question. The auditor therefore listens as to a lecture, without passion, without anxiety.

The song of Comus has airiness and jollity; but, what may recommend Milton's morals as well as his poetry, the invitations to pleasure are so general that they excite no distinct images of corrupt enjoyment and take no dangerous hold on the fancy.

The following soliloquies of Comus and the Lady are elegant but tedious. The song must owe much to the voice, if it ever can delight. At last the brothers enter with too much tranquillity; and when they have feared lest their sister should be in danger and hoped that she is not in danger, the Elder makes a speech in praise of chastity, and the Younger finds how fine it is to be a philosopher.

Then descends the Spirit in form of a shepherd; and the brother, instead of being in haste to ask his help, praises his singing and inquires his business in that place. It is remarkable that at this interview the brother is taken with a short fit of rhyming. The Spirit

---

[10] Sentence.

relates that the Lady is in the power of Comus, the brother moralizes again, and the Spirit makes a long narration, of no use because it is false and therefore unsuitable to a good being.

In all these parts the language is poetical and the sentiments are generous, but there is something wanting to allure attention.

The dispute between the Lady and Comus is the most animated and affecting scene of the drama and wants nothing but a brisker reciprocation of objections and replies to invite attention and detain it.

The songs are vigorous and full of imagery, but they are harsh in their diction and not very musical in their numbers.

Throughout the whole the figures[11] are too bold and the language too luxuriant for dialogue. It is a drama in the epic style, inelegantly splendid and tediously instructive.

The *Sonnets* were written in different parts of Milton's life upon different occasions. They deserve not any particular criticism, for of the best it can only be said that they are not bad, and perhaps only the eighth and the twenty-first are truly entitled to this slender commendation. The fabric of a sonnet, however adapted to the Italian language, has never succeeded in ours which, having greater variety of termination, requires the rhymes to be often changed.

Those little pieces may be dispatched without much anxiety; a greater work calls for greater care. I am now to examine *Paradise Lost,* a poem which, considered with respect to design, may claim the first place and with respect to performance the second[12] among the productions of the human mind.

By the general consent of critics the first praise of genius is due to the writer of an epic poem as it requires an assemblage of all the powers which are singly sufficient for other compositions. Poetry is the art of uniting pleasure with truth by calling imagination to the help of reason. Epic poetry undertakes to teach the most important truths by the most pleasing precepts and therefore relates some great event in the most affecting manner. History must supply the writer with the rudiments of narration, which he must improve and exalt by a nobler art, animate by dramatic energy, and diversify by retrospection and anticipation; morality must teach him the exact bounds and different

---

[11] Figurative language.

[12] Presumably second only to Homer's *Iliad*.

shades of vice and virtue; from policy and the practice of life he has to learn the discriminations of character and the tendency of the passions, either single or combined; and physiology[13] must supply him with illustrations and images. To put these materials to poetical use is required an imagination capable of painting nature and realizing fiction. Nor is he yet a poet till he has attained the whole extension of his language, distinguished all the delicacies of phrase and all the colors of words, and learned to adjust their different sounds to all the varieties of metrical modulation.

Bossu is of opinion that the poet's first work is to find a *moral*, which his fable is afterwards to illustrate and establish. This seems to have been the process only of Milton: the moral of other poems is incidental and consequent; in Milton's only it is essential and intrinsic. His purpose was the most useful and the most arduous: "to vindicate the ways of God to man," to show the reasonableness of religion and the necessity of obedience to the Divine Law.

To convey this moral there must be a *fable*, a narration artfully constructed so as to excite curiosity and surprise expectation. In this part of his work Milton must be confessed to have equaled every other poet. He has involved in his account of the Fall of Man the events which preceded and those that were to follow it; he has interwoven the whole system of theology with such propriety that every part appears to be necessary and scarcely any recital is wished shorter for the sake of quickening the progress of the main action.

The subject of an epic poem is naturally an event of great importance. That of Milton is not the destruction of a city, the conduct of a colony, or the foundation of an empire. His subject is the fate of worlds, the revolutions of heaven and earth; rebellion against the Supreme King raised by the highest order of created beings; the overthrow of their host and the punishment of their crime; the creation of a new race of reasonable creatures; their original happiness and innocence, their forfeiture of immortality, and their restoration to hope and peace.

Great events can be hastened or retarded only by persons of elevated dignity. Before the greatness displayed in Milton's poem all other greatness shrinks away. The weakest of his agents are the

---

[13] Natural science.

highest and noblest of human beings, the original parents of mankind, with whose actions the elements consented, on whose rectitude or deviation of will depended the state of terrestrial nature and the condition of all the future inhabitants of the globe.

Of the other agents in the poem, the chief are such as it is irreverence to name on slight occasions. The rest are lower powers,

> of which the least could wield
> Those elements, and arm him with the force
> Of all their regions,

powers which only the control of Omnipotence restrains from laying creation waste and filling the vast expanse of space with ruin and confusion. To display the motives and actions of beings thus superior, so far as human reason can examine them or human imagination represent them, is the task which this mighty poet has undertaken and performed.

In the examination of epic poems much speculation is commonly employed upon the *characters*. The characters in the *Paradise Lost* which admit of examination are those of angels and of man: of angels good and evil, of man in his innocent and sinful state.

Among the angels the virtue of Raphael is mild and placid, of easy condescension[14] and free communication; that of Michael is regal and lofty and, as may seem, attentive to the dignity of his own nature. Abdiel and Gabriel appear occasionally and act as every incident requires; the solitary fidelity of Abdiel is very amiably painted.

Of the evil angels the characters are more diversified. To Satan, as Addison observes, such sentiments are given as suit "the most exalted and most depraved being." Milton has been censured by Clark, for the impiety which sometimes breaks from Satan's mouth. For there are thoughts, as he justly remarks, which no observation of character can justify because no good man would willingly permit them to pass, however transiently, through his own mind. To make Satan speak as a rebel without any such expressions as might taint the reader's imagination was indeed one of the great difficulties in Milton's undertaking, and I cannot but think that he has extricated

[14] Affability with inferiors.

himself with great happiness. There is in Satan's speeches little that can give pain to a pious ear. The language of rebellion cannot be the same with that of obedience. The malignity of Satan foams in haughtiness and obstinacy, but his expressions are commonly general and no otherwise offensive than as they are wicked.

The other chiefs of the celestial rebellion are very judiciously discriminated in the first and second books, and the ferocious character of Moloch appears both in the battle and the council with exact consistency.

To Adam and to Eve are given during their innocence such sentiments as innocence can generate and utter. Their love is pure benevolence and mutual veneration; their repasts are without luxury and their diligence without toil. Their addresses to their Maker have little more than the voice of admiration and gratitude. Fruition left them nothing to ask, and innocence left them nothing to fear.

But with guilt enter distrust and discord, mutual accusation, and stubborn self-defense; they regard each other with alienated minds and dread their Creator as the avenger of their transgression. At last they seek shelter in his mercy, soften to repentance, and melt in supplication. Both before and after the Fall the superiority of Adam is diligently sustained.

Of the *probable* and the *marvelous,* two parts of a vulgar epic poem which immerge[15] the critic in deep consideration, the *Paradise Lost* requires little to be said. It contains the history of a miracle, of Creation and Redemption; it displays the power and the mercy of the Supreme Being; the probable therefore is marvelous, and the marvelous is probable. The substance of the narrative is truth; and as truth allows no choice, it is like necessity superior to rule. To the accidental or adventitious parts, as to everything human, some slight exceptions may be made. But the main fabric is immovably supported.

It is justly remarked by Addison that this poem has by the nature of its subject the advantage above all others that it is universally and perpetually interesting. All mankind will, through all ages, bear the same relation to Adam and to Eve, and must partake of that good and evil which extend to themselves.

---

[15] Vulgar : normal, secular; immerge : plunge.

Of the *machinery*, . . . by which is meant the occasional interposition of supernatural power, another fertile topic of critical remarks, here is no room to speak because everything is done under the immediate and visible direction of Heaven, but the rule is so far observed that no part of the action could have been accomplished by any other means.

Of *episodes,*[16] I think there are only two, contained in Raphael's relation of the war in heaven and Michael's prophetic account of the changes to happen in this world. Both are closely connected with the great action; one was necessary to Adam as a warning, the other as a consolation.

To the completeness or *integrity* of the design nothing can be objected; it has distinctly and clearly what Aristotle requires, a beginning, a middle, and an end. There is perhaps no poem of the same length from which so little can be taken without apparent mutilation. Here are no funeral games, nor is there any long description of a shield.[17] The short digressions at the beginning of the third, seventh, and ninth books might doubtless be spared; but superfluities so beautiful who would take away? or who does not wish that the author of the *Iliad* had gratified succeeding ages with a little knowledge of himself? Perhaps no passages are more frequently or more attentively read than those extrinsic paragraphs, and since the end of poetry is pleasure, that cannot be unpoetical with which all are pleased.

The questions whether the action of the poem be strictly *one,* whether the poem can be properly termed *heroic*, and who is the hero, are raised by such readers as draw their principles of judgment rather from books than from reason. Milton, though he entitled *Paradise Lost* only a *poem,* yet calls it himself *heroic song.* Dryden petulantly and indecently denies the heroism of Adam because he was overcome, but there is no reason why the hero should not be unfortunate except established practice, since success and virtue do not go necessarily together. Cato is the hero of Lucan, but Lucan's authority will not be suffered by Quintilian to decide.[18] However, if success be necessary,

[16] Digressions.

[17] These appear in Homer's *Iliad* and Vergil's *Aeneid.*

[18] Lucan in his *Pharsalia* (65 A.D.) showed Cato fighting on the losing side—a topic Quintilian felt more suitable for orators than poets (*Institutes,* X,i,90).

Adam's deceiver was at last crushed; Adam was restored to his Maker's favor and therefore may securely resume his human rank.

After the scheme and fabric of the poem must be considered its component parts, the sentiments and the diction.

The *sentiments,* as expressive of manners or appropriated to characters, are for the greater part unexceptionably just.

Splendid passages containing lessons of morality or precepts of prudence occur seldom. Such is the original formation of this poem that as it admits no human manners till the Fall, it can give little assistance to human conduct. Its end is to raise the thoughts above sublunary cares or pleasures. Yet the praise of that fortitude with which Abdiel maintained his singularity of virtue against the scorn of multitudes may be accommodated to all times, and Raphael's reproof of Adam's curiosity after the planetary motions with the answer returned by Adam may be confidently opposed[19] to any rule of life which any poet has delivered.

The thoughts which are occasionally called forth in the progress are such as could only be produced by an imagination in the highest degree fervid and active, to which materials were supplied by incessant study and unlimited curiosity. The heat of Milton's mind might be said to sublimate his learning, to throw off into his work the spirit of science unmingled with its grosser parts.

He had considered creation in its whole extent, and his descriptions are therefore learned. He had accustomed his imagination to unrestrained indulgence, and his conceptions therefore were extensive. The characteristic quality of his poem is sublimity. He sometimes descends to the elegant, but his element is the great. He can occasionally invest himself with grace, but his natural port[20] is gigantic loftiness. He can please when pleasure is required, but it is his peculiar power to astonish.

He seems to have been well acquainted with his own genius and to know what it was that nature had bestowed upon him more bountifully than upon others: the power of displaying the vast, illuminating the splendid, enforcing the awful, darkening the gloomy, and aggra-

---

[19] Set beside, compared.

[20] Deportment, style. In this passage, Johnson is contrasting the sublime with the beautiful (see Chapter 2. n.2).

vating the dreadful; he therefore chose a subject on which too much could not be said, on which he might tire his fancy without the censure of extravagance.

The appearances of nature and the occurrences of life did not satiate his appetite of greatness. To paint things as they are requires a minute attention and employs the memory rather than the fancy. Milton's delight was to sport in the wide regions of possibility; reality was a scene too narrow for his mind. He sent his faculties out upon discovery into worlds where only imagination can travel, and delighted to form new modes of existence and furnish sentiment and action to superior beings, to trace the counsels of hell or accompany the choirs of heaven.

But he could not be always in other worlds; he must sometimes revisit earth and tell of things visible and known. When he cannot raise wonder by the sublimity of his mind, he gives delight by its fertility.

Whatever be his subject, he never fails to fill the imagination. But his images and descriptions of the scenes or operations of nature do not seem to be always copied from original form nor to have the freshness, raciness, and energy of immediate observation. He saw nature, as Dryden expresses it, "through the spectacles of books," and on most occasions calls learning to his assistance. The garden of Eden brings to his mind the vale of Enna where Proserpine was gathering flowers. Satan makes his way through fighting elements like Argo between the Cyanean rocks or Ulysses between the two Sicilian whirlpools when he shunned Charybdis on the *larboard.* The mythological allusions have been justly censured as not being always used with notice of their vanity, but they contribute variety to the narration and produce an alternate exercise of the memory and the fancy.

His similes are less numerous and more various than those of his predecessors. But he does not confine himself within the limits of rigorous comparison; his great excellence is amplitude, and he expands the adventitious image beyond the dimensions which the occasion required. Thus, comparing the shield of Satan to the orb of the Moon, he crowds the imagination with the discovery of the telescope and all the wonders which the telescope discovers.

Of his moral sentiments it is hardly praise to affirm that they excel those of all other poets; for this superiority he was indebted to his acquaintance with the sacred writings. The ancient epic poets, wanting the light of Revelation, were very unskillful teachers of virtue; their principal characters may be great, but they are not amiable. The reader may rise from their works with a greater degree of active or passive fortitude and sometimes of prudence, but he will be able to carry away few precepts of justice and none of mercy.

From the Italian writers it appears that the advantages of even Christian knowledge may be possessed in vain. Ariosto's pravity[21] is generally known; and though the *Deliverance of Jerusalem* may be considered as a sacred subject, the poet[22] has been very sparing of moral instruction.

In Milton every line breathes sanctity of thought and purity of manners except when the train of the narration requires the introduction of the rebellious spirits, and even they are compelled to acknowledge their subjection to God in such a manner as excites reverence and confirms piety.

Of human beings there are but two, but those two are the parents of mankind, venerable before their fall for dignity and innocence and amiable after it for repentance and submission. In their first state their affection is tender without weakness and their piety sublime without presumption. When they have sinned, they show how discord begins in mutual frailty and how it ought to cease in mutual forbearance; how confidence of the divine favor is forfeited by sin, and how hope of pardon may be obtained by penitence and prayer. A state of innocence we can only conceive, if indeed in our present misery it be possible to conceive it; but the sentiments and worship proper to a fallen and offending being we have all to learn as we have all to practice.

The poet, whatever be done, is always great. Our progenitors in their first state conversed with angels; even when folly and sin had degraded them, they had not in their humiliation "the port of mean suitors," and they rise again to reverential regard when we find that their prayers were heard.

As human passions did not enter the world before the Fall, there is in the *Paradise Lost* little opportunity for the pathetic, but what lit-

[21] Depravity.

[22] Torquato Tasso.

tle there is has not been lost. That passion which is peculiar to rational nature, the anguish arising from the consciousness of transgression and the horrors attending the sense of the divine displeasure, are very justly described and forcibly impressed. But the passions are moved only on one occasion; sublimity is the general prevailing quality in this poem—sublimity variously modified, sometimes descriptive, sometimes argumentative.

The defects and faults of *Paradise Lost,* for faults and defects every work of man must have, it is the business of impartial criticism to discover. As in displaying the excellence of Milton I have not made long quotations because of selecting beauties there had been no end, I shall in the same general manner mention that which seems to deserve censure, for what Englishman can take delight in transcribing passages which, if they lessen the reputation of Milton, diminish in some degree the honor of our country? . . .

The plan of *Paradise Lost* has this inconvenience, that it comprises neither human actions nor human manners. The man and woman who act and suffer are in a state which no other man or woman can ever know. The reader finds no transaction in which he can be engaged, beholds no condition in which he can by any effort of imagination place himself; he has, therefore, little natural curiosity or sympathy.

We all, indeed, feel the effects of Adam's disobedience; we all sin like Adam and like him must all bewail our offenses; we have restless and insidious enemies in the fallen angels, and in the blessed spirits we have guardians and friends; in the redemption of mankind we hope to be included, and in the description of heaven and hell we are surely interested as we are all to reside hereafter either in the regions of horror or of bliss.

But these truths are too important to be new; they have been taught to our infancy; they have mingled with our solitary thoughts and familiar conversation and are habitually interwoven with the whole texture of life. Being therefore not new, they raise no unaccustomed emotion in the mind; what we knew before we cannot learn; what is not unexpected cannot surprise.

Of the ideas suggested by these awful scenes, from some we recede with reverence except when stated hours require their association, and from others we shrink with horror or admit them only as salutary inflictions, as counterpoises to our interests and passions. Such images rather obstruct the career of fancy than incite it.

Pleasure and terror are indeed the genuine sources of poetry, but poetical pleasure must be such as human imagination can at least conceive and poetical terror such as human strength and fortitude may combat. The good and evil of eternity are too ponderous for the wings of wit; the mind sinks under them in passive helplessness, content with calm belief and humble adoration.

Known truths, however, may take a different appearance and be conveyed to the mind by a new train of intermediate images. This Milton has undertaken and performed with pregnancy and vigor of mind peculiar to himself. Whoever considers the few radical[23] positions which the Scriptures afforded him will wonder by what energetic operation he expanded them to such extent and ramified them to so much variety, restrained as he was by religious reverence from licentiousness[24] of fiction.

Here is a full display of the united force of study and genius, of a great accumulation of materials with judgment to digest and fancy to combine them; Milton was able to select from nature or from story, from ancient fable or from modern science, whatever could illustrate or adorn his thoughts. An accumulation of knowledge impregnated his mind, fermented by study and sublimed by imagination.

It has been therefore said, without an indecent hyperbole, by one of his encomiasts that in reading *Paradise Lost* we read a book of universal knowledge.

But original deficience cannot be supplied. The want of human interest is always felt. *Paradise Lost* is one of the books which the reader admires and lays down and forgets to take up again. None ever wished it longer than it is. Its perusal is a duty rather than a pleasure. We read Milton for instruction, retire harassed and overburdened, and look elsewhere for recreation; we desert our master and seek for companions.

Another inconvenience of Milton's design is that it requires the description of what cannot be described, the agency of spirits. He saw

---

[23] Root, basic.

[24] Excessive freedom.

that immateriality supplied no images and that he could not show angels acting but by instruments of action; he therefore invested them with form and matter. This, being necessary, was therefore defensible, and he should have secured the consistency of his system by keeping immateriality out of sight and enticing his reader to drop it from his thoughts. But he has unhappily perplexed his poetry with his philosophy. His infernal and celestial powers are sometimes pure spirit and sometimes animated body. When Satan walks with his lance upon the "burning marl," he has a body; when in his passage between hell and the new world he is in danger of sinking in the vacuity and is supported by a gust of rising vapors, he has a body; when he animates the toad, he seems to be mere spirit that can penetrate matter at pleasure; when he "starts up in his own shape," he has at least a determined form; and when he is brought before Gabriel, he has "a spear and a shield" which he had the power of hiding in the toad though the arms of the contending angels are evidently material.

The vulgar inhabitants of Pandaemonium, being "incorporeal spirits," are "at large though without number" in a limited space; yet in the battle when they were overwhelmed by mountains, their armor hurt them, "crushed in upon their substance, now grown gross by sinning." This likewise happened to the uncorrupted angels, who were overthrown "the sooner for their arms, for unarmed they might easily as spirits have evaded by contraction or remove." Even as spirits they are hardly spiritual, for "contraction" and "remove" are images of matter, but if they could have escaped without their armor, they might have escaped from it and left only the empty cover to be battered. Uriel, when he rides on a sunbeam, is material; Satan is material when he is afraid of the prowess of Adam.

The confusion of spirit and matter which pervades the whole narration of the war of heaven fills it with incongruity, and the book in which it is related is, I believe, the favorite of children and gradually neglected as knowledge is increased.

After the operation of immaterial agents which cannot be explained may be considered that of allegorical persons, which have no real existence. To exalt causes into agents, to invest abstract ideas with form and animate them with activity has always been the right of poetry. But such airy beings are for the most part suffered only to do their natural office and retire. Thus Fame tells a tale, and Victory hovers over a general or perches on a standard, but Fame and Victory can do no more. To give them any real employment or ascribe to them any material agency is to make them allegorical no longer but to shock the mind by ascribing effects to nonentity. In the *Prometheus* of Aeschylus we see Violence and Strength and in the *Alcestis* of Euripides we see Death brought upon the stage, all as active persons of the drama, but no precedents can justify absurdity.

Milton's allegory of Sin and Death is undoubtedly faulty. Sin is indeed the mother of Death and may be allowed to be the portress of hell; but when they stop the journey of Satan, a journey described as real, and when Death offers him battle, the allegory is broken. That Sin and Death should have shown the way to hell might have been allowed, but they cannot facilitate the passage by building a bridge because the difficulty of Satan's passage is described as real and sensible[25] and the bridge ought to be only figurative. The hell assigned to the rebellious spirits is described as not less local than the residence of man. It is placed in some distant part of space, separated from the regions of harmony and order by a chaotic waste and an unoccupied vacuity; but Sin and Death worked up a "mole of aggravated soil" cemented with "asphaltus," a work too bulky for ideal architects.

This unskillful allegory appears to me one of the greatest faults of the poem, and to this there was no temptation but[26] the author's opinion of its beauty.

To the conduct of the narrative some objections may be made. Satan is with great expectation brought before Gabriel in Paradise and is suffered to go away unmolested. The creation of man is represented as the consequence of the vacuity left in heaven by the expulsion of the rebels, yet Satan mentions it as a report "rife in heaven" before his departure.

To find sentiments for the state of innocence was very difficult, and something of anticipation perhaps is now and then discovered. Adam's discourse of dreams seems not to be the speculation of a new-created being. I know not whether his answer to the angel's reproof for curiosity does not want something of propriety; it is the speech of a man acquainted with many other men. Some philosophical notions,

[25] Perceptible to the senses.

[26] Except for.

especially when the philosophy is false, might have been better omitted. The angel, in a comparison, speaks of "timorous deer" before deer were yet timorous and before Adam could understand the comparison.

Dryden remarks that Milton has some flats among his elevations. This is only to say that all the parts are not equal. In every work one part must be for the sake of others; a palace must have passages, a poem must have transitions. It is no more to be required that wit should always be blazing than that the sun should always stand at noon. In a great work there is a vicissitude of luminous and opaque parts as there is in the world a succession of day and night. Milton, when he has expatiated[27] in the sky, may be allowed sometimes to revisit earth, for what other author ever soared so high or sustained his flight so long?

Milton, being well versed in the Italian poets, appears to have borrowed often from them; and as every man catches something from his companions, his desire of imitating Ariosto's levity has disgraced his work with the "Paradise of Fools," a fiction not in itself ill-imagined but too ludicrous for its place.

His play on words, in which he delights too often; his equivocations,[28] which Bentley endeavors to defend by the example of the ancients; his unnecessary and ungraceful use of terms of art[29] it is not necessary to mention because they are easily remarked and generally censured and at last bear so little proportion to the whole that they scarcely deserve the attention of a critic.

Such are the faults of that wonderful performance, *Paradise Lost,* which he who can put in balance with its beauties must be considered not as nice but as dull, as less to be censured for want of candor[30] than pitied for want of sensibility.

Of *Paradise Regained* the general judgment seems now to be right, that it is in many parts elegant and everywhere instructive. It was not to be supposed that the writer of *Paradise Lost* could ever write without great effusions of fancy and exalted precepts of wisdom.

[27] Walked or wandered about.

[28] Double meanings.

[29] Technical terms.

[30] Nice: discriminating; want of candor: lack of impartiality or kindness.

The basis of *Paradise Regained* is narrow; a dialogue without action can never please like an union of the narrative and dramatic powers. Had this poem been written not by Milton but by some imitator, it would have claimed and received universal praise.

If *Paradise Regained* has been too much depreciated, *Samson Agonistes* has in requital been too much admired. It could only be by long prejudice and the bigotry of learning that Milton could prefer the ancient tragedies with their encumbrance of a chorus to the exhibitions of the French and English stages, and it is only by a blind confidence in the reputation of Milton that a drama can be praised in which the intermediate parts have neither cause nor consequence, neither hasten nor retard the catastrophe.

In this tragedy are, however, many particular beauties, many just sentiments and striking lines, but it wants that power of attracting the attention which a well-connected plan produces.

Milton would not have excelled in dramatic writing; he knew human nature only in the gross and had never studied the shades of character nor the combinations of concurring or the perplexity of contending passions. He had read much and knew what books could teach, but had mingled little in the world and was deficient in the knowledge which experience must confer.

Through all his greater works there prevails an uniform peculiarity of *diction*, a mode and cast of expression which bears little resemblance to that of any former writer and which is so far removed from common use that an unlearned reader, when he first opens his book, finds himself surprised by a new language.

This novelty has been, by those who can find nothing wrong in Milton, imputed to his laborious endeavors after words suitable to the grandeur of his ideas. "Our language," says Addison, "sunk under him." But the truth is that both in prose and verse he had formed his style by a perverse and pedantic principle. He was desirous to use English words with a foreign idiom. This in all his prose is discovered and condemned, for there judgment operates freely, neither softened by the beauty nor awed by the dignity of his thoughts; but such is the power of his poetry that his call is obeyed without resistance, the reader feels himself in captivity to a higher and a nobler mind, and criticism sinks in admiration.

Milton's style was not modified by his subject; what is shown with greater extent in *Paradise Lost* may be found in *Comus*. One source of his peculiarity was his familiarity with the Tuscan poets; the disposition of his words is, I think, frequently Italian, perhaps sometimes combined with other tongues. Of him, at last, may be said what Jonson says of Spenser, that "he wrote no language" but has formed what Butler calls a "Babylonish dialect," in itself harsh and barbarous but made by exalted genius and extensive learning the vehicle of so much instruction and so much pleasure that, like other lovers, we find grace in its deformity.

Whatever be the faults of his diction, he cannot want the praise of copiousness and variety; he was master of his language in its full extent and has selected the melodious words with such diligence that from his book alone the art of English poetry might be learned.

After his diction, something must be said of his versification. "The measure," he says, "is the English heroic verse without rhyme."[31] Of this mode he had many examples among the Italians and some in his own country. The Earl of Surrey is said to have translated one of Virgil's books without rhyme, and besides our tragedies a few short poems had appeared in blank verse, particularly one tending to reconcile the nation to Raleigh's wild attempt upon Guiana and probably written by Raleigh himself. These petty performances cannot be supposed to have much influenced Milton, who more probably took his hint from Trissino's *Italia Liberata* and, finding blank verse easier than rhyme, was desirous of persuading himself that it is better.

"Rhyme," he says, and says truly, "is no necessary adjunct of true poetry." But perhaps of poetry as a mental operation meter or music is no necessary adjunct; it is, however, by the music of meter that poetry has been discriminated in all languages, and in languages melodiously constructed, by a due proportion of long and short syllables, meter is sufficient. But one language cannot communicate its rules to another; where meter is scanty and imperfect, some help is necessary. The music of the English heroic line strikes the ear so faintly that it is easily lost unless all the syllables of every line cooperate together; this cooperation can be only obtained by the

[31] In the Preface to *Paradise Lost*.

preservation of every verse unmingled with another as a distinct system of sounds, and this distinctness is obtained and preserved by the artifice of rhyme. The variety of pauses so much boasted by the lovers of blank verse changes the measures of an English poet to the periods of a declaimer, and there are only a few skillful and happy readers of Milton who enable their audience to perceive where the lines end or begin. "Blank verse," said an ingenious critic, "seems to be verse only to the eye."

Poetry may subsist without rhyme, but English poetry will not often please; nor can rhyme ever be safely spared but where the subject is able to support itself. Blank verse makes some approach to that which is called the *lapidary style,* has neither the easiness of prose nor the melody of numbers, and therefore tires by long continuance. Of the Italian writers without rhyme whom Milton alleges as precedents,[32] not one is popular; what reason could urge in its defense has been confuted by the ear.

But whatever be the advantage of rhyme, I cannot prevail on myself to wish that Milton had been a rhymer, for I cannot wish his work to be other than it is; yet like other heroes he is to be admired rather than imitated. He that thinks himself capable of astonishing may write blank verse, but those that hope only to please must condescend to rhyme.

The highest praise of genius is original invention. Milton cannot be said to have contrived the structure of an epic poem and therefore owes reverence to that vigor and amplitude of mind to which all generations must be indebted for the art of poetical narration, for the texture of the fable, the variation of incidents, the interposition of dialogue, and all the stratagems that surprise and enchain attention. But of all the borrowers from Homer, Milton is perhaps the least indebted. He was naturally a thinker for himself, confident of his own abilities and disdainful of help or hindrance; he did not refuse admission to the thoughts or images of his predecessors, but he did not seek them. From his contemporaries he neither courted nor received support; there is in his writings nothing by which the pride of other authors might be gratified or favor gained, no exchange of praise nor

---

[32] Ibid.

solicitation of support. His great works were performed under discountenance[33] and in blindness, but difficulties vanished at his touch; he was born for whatever is arduous, and his work is not the greatest of heroic poems only because it is not the first.

POPE

Of his intellectual character[34] the constituent and fundamental principle was good sense, a prompt and intuitive perception of consonance and propriety. He saw immediately of his own conceptions what was to be chosen and what to be rejected, and in the works of others what was to be shunned and what was to be copied.

But good sense alone is a sedate and quiescent quality, which manages its possessions well but does not increase them; it collects few materials for its own operations and preserves safety but never gains supremacy. Pope had likewise genius: a mind active, ambitious, and adventurous, always investigating, always aspiring; in its widest searches still longing to go forward, in its highest flights still wishing to be higher; always imagining something greater than it knows, always endeavoring more than it can do.

To assist these powers he is said to have had great strength and exactness of memory. That which he had heard or read was not easily lost, and he had before him not only what his own meditation suggested but what he had found in other writers that might be accommodated to his present purpose.

These benefits of nature he improved by incessant and unwearied diligence; he had recourse to every source of intelligence and lost no opportunity of information; he consulted the living as well as the dead; he read his compositions to his friends and was never content with mediocrity when excellence could be attained. He considered

---

[33] Discouragement.

[34] Pope's intellectual qualities are the last traits covered in a general analysis of Pope's "person," which follows the biographical section and precedes the critical appraisal of the poems. Although Johnson was supposed to write only a brief Preface, the *Life of Pope* took a whole volume in the new edition of the poet's work.

poetry as the business of his life, and however he might seem to lament his occupation, he followed it with constancy: to make verses was his first labor and to mend them was his last.

From his attention to poetry he was never diverted. If conversation offered anything that could be improved, he committed it to paper; if a thought, or perhaps an expression more happy than was common rose to his mind, he was careful to write it; an independent distich[35] was preserved for an opportunity of insertion, and some little fragments have been found containing lines or parts of lines to be wrought upon at some other time.

He was one of those few whose labor is their pleasure; he was never elevated to negligence nor wearied to impatience; he never passed a fault unamended by indifference nor quitted it by despair. He labored his works first to gain reputation and afterwards to keep it.

Of composition there are different methods. Some employ at once memory and invention, and, with little intermediate use of the pen, form and polish large masses by continued meditation and write their productions only when, in their own opinion, they have completed them. It is related of Virgil that his custom was to pour out a great number of verses in the morning and pass the day in retrenching exuberances and correcting inaccuracies. The method of Pope, as may be collected from his translation, was to write his first thoughts in his first words and gradually to amplify, decorate, rectify, and refine them.

With such faculties and such dispositions, he excelled every other writer in *poetical prudence;* he wrote in such a manner as might expose him to few hazards. He used almost always the same fabric of verse; and, indeed, by those few essays[36] which he made of any other he did not enlarge his reputation. Of this uniformity the certain consequence was readiness and dexterity. By perpetual practice language had in his mind a systematical arrangement; having always the same use for words, he had words so selected and combined as to be ready at his call. This increase of facility he confessed himself to have perceived in the progress of his translation.

---

[35] A unit of two lines, a couplet.

[36] Trials, attempts.

But what was yet of more importance, his effusions were always voluntary and his subjects chosen by himself. His independence secured him from drudging at a task and laboring upon a barren topic: he never exchanged praise for money nor opened a shop of condolence or congratulation. His poems, therefore, were scarce ever temporary.[37] He suffered coronations and royal marriages to pass without a song and derived no opportunities from recent events nor any popularity from the accidental disposition of his readers. He was never reduced to the necessity of soliciting the sun to shine upon a birthday, of calling the Graces and Virtues to a wedding, or of saying what multitudes have said before him. When he could produce nothing new, he was at liberty to be silent.

His publications were for the same reason never hasty. He is said to have sent nothing to the press till it had lain two years under his inspection; it is at least certain that he ventured nothing without nice[38] examination. He suffered the tumult of imagination to subside and the novelties of invention to grow familiar. He knew that the mind is always enamored of its own productions and did not trust his first fondness. He consulted his friends and listened with great willingness to criticism, and what was of more importance, he consulted himself and let nothing pass against his own judgment.

He professed to have learned his poetry from Dryden, whom, whenever an opportunity was presented, he praised through his whole life with unvaried liberality; and perhaps his character may receive some illustration if he be compared with his master.

Integrity of understanding and nicety of discernment were not allotted in a less proportion to Dryden than to Pope. The rectitude of Dryden's mind was sufficiently shown by the dismission of his poetical prejudices[39] and the rejection of unnatural thoughts and rugged numbers. But Dryden never desired to apply all the judgment that he had. He wrote, and professed to write, merely for the people; and when he pleased others, he contented himself. He spent no time in struggles to rouse latent powers; he never attempted to make that better which

---

[37] Written for a specific occasion and hence time-bound.

[38] Precise.

[39] Rejection of his poetic preferences.

was already good nor often to mend what he must have known to be faulty. He wrote, as he tells us, with very little consideration; when occasion or necessity called upon him, he poured out what the present moment happened to supply and, when once it had passed the press, ejected it from his mind, for when he had no pecuniary interest, he had no further solicitude.

Pope was not content to satisfy; he desired to excel and therefore always endeavored to do his best; he did not court the candor[40] but dared the judgment of his reader and, expecting no indulgence from others, he showed none to himself. He examined lines and words with minute and punctilious observation and retouched every part with indefatigable diligence till he had left nothing to be forgiven.

For this reason he kept his pieces very long in his hands while he considered and reconsidered them. The only poems which can be supposed to have been written with such regard to the times as might hasten their publication were the two satires of *Thirty-eight*,[41] of which Dodsley told me that they were brought to him by the author that they might be fairly copied. "Almost every line," he said, "was then written twice over; I gave him a clean transcript, which he sent some time afterwards to me for the press with every line written twice over a second time."

His declaration that his care for his works ceased at their publication was not strictly true. His parental attention never abandoned them; what he found amiss in the first edition he silently corrected in those that followed. He appears to have revised the *Iliad* and freed it from some of its imperfections, and the *Essay on Criticism* received many improvements after its first appearance. It will seldom be found that he altered without adding clearness, elegance, or vigor. Pope had perhaps the judgment of Dryden, but Dryden certainly wanted the diligence of Pope.

In acquired knowledge the superiority must be allowed to Dryden, whose education was more scholastic[42] and who before he became an author had been allowed more time for study with better

---

[40] Kindness.

[41] 1738: Dialogues I and II, now called *Epilogue to the Satires*.

[42] Scholarly, university trained.

means of information. His mind has a larger range, and he collects his images and illustrations from a more extensive circumference of science. Dryden knew more of man in his general nature, and Pope in his local manners. The notions of Dryden were formed by comprehensive speculation, and those of Pope by minute attention. There is more dignity in the knowledge of Dryden, and more certainty in that of Pope.

Poetry was not the sole praise of either, for both excelled likewise in prose, but Pope did not borrow his prose from his predecessor. The style of Dryden is capricious and varied, that of Pope is cautious and uniform; Dryden obeys the motions of his own mind, Pope constrains his mind to his own rules of composition. Dryden is sometimes vehement and rapid; Pope is always smooth, uniform, and gentle. Dryden's page is a natural field, rising into inequalities and diversified by the varied exuberance of abundant vegetation; Pope's is a velvet lawn, shaven by the scythe and leveled by the roller.

Of genius—that power which constitutes a poet, that quality without which judgment is cold and knowledge is inert, that energy which collects, combines, amplifies, and animates—the superiority must, with some hesitation, be allowed to Dryden. It is not to be inferred that of this poetical vigor Pope had only a little because Dryden had more, for every other writer since Milton must give place to Pope; and even of Dryden it must be said that if he has brighter paragraphs, he has not better poems. Dryden's performances were always hasty, either excited by some external occasion or extorted by domestic necessity; he composed without consideration and published without correction. What his mind could supply at call or gather in one excursion was all that he sought and all that he gave. The dilatory caution of Pope enabled him to condense his sentiments, to multiply his images, and to accumulate all that study might produce or chance might supply. If the flights of Dryden therefore are higher, Pope continues longer on the wing. If of Dryden's fire the blaze is brighter, of Pope's the heat is more regular and constant. Dryden often surpasses expectation, and Pope never falls below it. Dryden is read with frequent astonishment and Pope with perpetual delight.

This parallel will, I hope, when it is well considered be found just; and if the reader should suspect me, as I suspect myself, of some partial fondness for the memory of Dryden, let him not too hastily condemn me, for meditation and inquiry may perhaps show him the reasonableness of my determination.

The works of Pope are now to be distinctly examined, not so much with attention to slight faults or petty beauties as to the general character and effect of each performance. . . .[43]

One of his greatest though of his earliest works is the *Essay on Criticism,* which, if he had written nothing else, would have placed him among the first critics and the first poets as it exhibits every mode of excellence that can embellish or dignify didactic composition: selection of matter, novelty of arrangement, justness of precept, splendor of illustration, and propriety of digression. I know not whether it be pleasing to consider that he produced this piece at twenty and never afterwards excelled it; he that delights himself with observing that such powers may be so soon attained cannot but grieve to think that life was ever after at a stand.

To mention the particular beauties of the *Essay* would be unprofitably tedious, but I cannot forbear to observe that the comparison of a student's progress in the sciences with the journey of a traveler in the Alps is perhaps the best that English poetry can show. A simile, to be perfect, must both illustrate and ennoble the subject, must show it to the understanding in a clearer view and display it to the fancy with greater dignity; but either of these qualities may be sufficient to recommend it. In didactic poetry, of which the great purpose is instruction, a simile may be praised which illustrates though it does not ennoble; in heroics, that may be admitted which ennobles though it does not illustrate. That it may be complete, it is required to exhibit, independently of its reference, a pleasing image, for a simile is said to be a short episode. To this antiquity was so attentive that circumstances were sometimes added which, having no parallels, served only to fill the imagination and produced what Perrault ludicrously called "comparisons with a long tail." In their similes the greatest writers have sometimes failed: the ship race, compared with the chariot race,

---

[43] Brief discussions of the *Pastorals, Windsor Forest,* and other early poems are omitted.

is neither illustrated nor aggrandized; land and water make all the difference: when Apollo running after Daphne is likened to a greyhound chasing a hare, there is nothing gained; the ideas of pursuit and flight are too plain to be made plainer, and a god and the daughter of a god are not represented much to their advantage by a hare and dog.[44] The simile of the Alps has no useless parts yet affords a striking picture by itself; it makes the foregoing position better understood and enables it to take faster hold on the attention; it assists the apprehension and elevates the fancy.

Let me likewise dwell a little on the celebrated paragraph in which it is directed that "the sound should seem an echo to the sense," a precept which Pope is allowed to have observed beyond any other English poet.

This notion of representative meter and the desire of discovering frequent adaptations of the sound to the sense have produced, in my opinion, many wild conceits[45] and imaginary beauties. All that can furnish this representation are the sounds of the words considered singly and the time in which they are pronounced. Every language has some words framed to exhibit the noises which they express, as *thump, rattle, growl, hiss*. These, however, are but few, and the poet cannot make them more, nor can they be of any use but when sound is to be mentioned. The time of pronunciation was in the dactylic measures of the learned languages[46] capable of considerable variety, but that variety could be accommodated only to motion or duration, and different degrees of motion were perhaps expressed by verses rapid or slow, without much attention of the writer, when the image had full possession of his fancy; but our language having little flexibility, our verses can differ very little in their cadence. The fancied resemblances, I fear, arise sometimes merely from the ambiguity of words; there is supposed to be some relation between a *soft* line and a *soft* couch or between *hard* syllables and *hard* fortune.

Motion, however, may be in some sort exemplified; and yet it may be suspected that even in such resemblances the mind often

---

[44] These similes appear in Virgil's *Aeneid* and Ovid's *Metamorphoses*.

[45] Fanciful notions.

[46] Classical languages: Greek and Latin.

governs the ear, and the sounds are estimated by their meaning. One of the most successful attempts has been to describe the labor of Sisyphus:

> With many a weary step, and many a groan,
> Up a high hill he heaves a huge round stone;
> The huge round stone, resulting with a bound,
> Thunders impetuous down, and smokes along the ground.[47]

Who does not perceive the stone to move slowly upward and roll violently back? But set the same numbers to another sense:

> While many a merry tale, and many a song,
> Cheered the rough road, we wished the rough road long.
> The rough road then, returning in a round,
> Mocked our impatient steps, for all was fairy ground.

We have now surely lost much of the delay and much of the rapidity.

But to show how little the greatest master of numbers can fix the principles of representative harmony, it will be sufficient to remark that the poet, who tells us that

> When Ajax strives—the words move slow:
> Not so when swift Camilla scours the plain,
> Flies o'er th' unbending corn, and skims along the main;[48]

when he had enjoyed for about thirty years the praise of Camilla's lightness of foot, tried another experiment upon *sound* and *time* and produced this memorable triplet:

> Waller was smooth; but Dryden taught to join
> The varying verse, the full resounding line,
> The long majestic march, and energy divine.

Here are the swiftness of the rapid race and the march of slow-paced majesty exhibited by the same poet in the same sequence of

---

[47] From Pope's trans. of the *Odyssey,* XI, 735 ff.; "resulting with a bound": rebounding.

[48] *An Essay on Criticism,* 11s. 370–73; the following quotation is from Pope's *Imitations of Horace, Epistles,* II, i, 267–69.

syllables except that the exact prosodist will find the line of *swiftness* by one time longer than that of *tardiness*.

Beauties of this kind are commonly fancied, and when real are technical and nugatory,[49] not to be rejected and not to be solicited.

To the praises which have been accumulated on *The Rape of the Lock* by readers of every class, from the critic to the waiting-maid, it is difficult to make any addition. Of that which is universally allowed to be the most attractive of all ludicrous[50] compositions, let it rather be now inquired from what sources the power of pleasing is derived.

Dr. Warburton, who excelled in critical perspicacity, has remarked that the preternatural agents are very happily adapted to the purposes of the poem. The heathen deities can no longer gain attention; we should have turned away from a contest between Venus and Diana. The employment of allegorical persons always excites conviction of its own absurdity; they may produce effects but cannot conduct actions; when the phantom is put in motion, it dissolves; thus Discord may raise a mutiny, but Discord cannot conduct a march nor besiege a town. Pope brought into view a new race of beings with powers and passions proportionate to their operation. The sylphs and gnomes act at the toilet and the tea table what more terrific and more powerful phantoms perform on the stormy ocean or the field of battle; they give their proper help and do their proper mischief.

Pope is said by an objector not to have been the inventor of this petty nation, a charge which might with more justice have been brought against the author of the *Iliad,* who doubtless adopted the religious system of his country; for what is there but the names of his agents which Pope has not invented? Has he not assigned them characters and operations never heard of before? Has he not, at least, given them their first poetical existence? If this is not sufficient to denominate his work original, nothing original ever can be written.

In this work are exhibited in a very high degree the two most engaging powers of an author. New things are made familiar, and familiar things are made new. A race of aerial people never heard of before is presented to us in a manner so clear and easy that the reader seeks for no further information but immediately mingles with his new

[49] Trifling.

[50] Comic.

acquaintance, adopts their interests and attends their pursuits, loves a sylph and detests a gnome.

That familiar things are made new every paragraph will prove. The subject of the poem is an event below the common incidents of common life; nothing real is introduced that is not seen so often as to be no longer regarded, yet the whole detail of a female day is here brought before us invested with so much art of decoration that, though nothing is disguised, everything is striking, and we feel all the appetite of curiosity for that from which we have a thousand times turned fastidiously away.

The purpose of the poet is, as he tells us, to laugh at "the little unguarded follies of the female sex." It is therefore without justice that Dennis charges *The Rape of the Lock* with the want of a moral and for that reason sets it below *The Lutrin,* which exposes the pride and discord of the clergy. Perhaps neither Pope nor Boileau has made the world much better than he found it; but if they had both succeeded, it were easy to tell who would have deserved most from public gratitude. The freaks and humors and spleen and vanity of women, as they embroil families in discord and fill houses with disquiet, do more to obstruct the happiness of life in a year than the ambition of the clergy in many centuries. It has been well observed that the misery of man proceeds not from any single crush of overwhelming evil but from small vexations continually repeated.

It is remarked by Dennis likewise that the machinery is superfluous, that by all the bustle of preternatural operation the main event is neither hastened nor retarded. To this charge an efficacious answer is not easily made. The sylphs cannot be said to help or to oppose, and it must be allowed to imply some want of art that their power has not been sufficiently intermingled with the action. Other parts may likewise be charged with want of connection; the game at *ombre*[51] might be spared, but if the lady had lost her hair while she was intent upon her cards, it might have been inferred that those who are too fond of play will be in danger of neglecting more important interests. Those perhaps are faults, but what are such faults to so much excellence!

---

[51] Card game dramatized in *The Rape of the Lock.*

The Epistle of *Eloise to Abelard* is one of the most happy productions of human wit; the subject is so judiciously chosen that it would be difficult, in turning over the annals of the world, to find another which so many circumstances concur to recommend. We regularly interest ourselves most in the fortune of those who most deserve our notice. Abelard and Eloise were conspicuous in their days for eminence of merit. The heart naturally loves truth. The adventures and misfortunes of this illustrious pair are known from undisputed history. Their fate does not leave the mind in hopeless dejection, for they both found quiet and consolation in retirement and piety. So new and so affecting is their story that it supersedes invention, and imagination ranges at full liberty without straggling into scenes of fable.

The story thus skillfully adopted has been diligently improved. Pope has left nothing behind him which seems more the effect of studious perseverance and laborious revisal. Here is particularly observable the *curiosa felicitas,*[52] a fruitful soil and careful cultivation. Here is no crudeness of sense nor asperity of language.

The sources from which sentiments which have so much vigor and efficacy have been drawn are shown to be the mystic writers by the learned author of the *Essay on the Life and Writings of Pope,*[53] a book which teaches how the brow of criticism may be smoothed and how she may be enabled with all her severity to attract and to delight.

The train of my disquisition has now conducted me to that poetical wonder, the translation of the *Iliad,* a performance which no age or nation can pretend to equal. To the Greeks translation was almost unknown; it was totally unknown to the inhabitants of Greece. They had no recourse to the Barbarians for poetical beauties but sought for everything in Homer, where, indeed, there is but little which they might not find.

The Italians have been very diligent translators; but I can hear of no version, unless perhaps Anguillara's Ovid may be excepted, which is read with eagerness. The *Iliad* of Salvini every reader may discover to be punctiliously exact; but it seems to be the work of a linguist skill-

---

[52] Diligent cultivation.

[53] Joseph Warton's.

fully pedantic, and his countrymen, the proper judges of its power to please, reject it with disgust.

Their predecessors, the Romans, have left some specimens of translation behind them, and that employment must have had some credit in which Tully and Germanicus engaged; but unless we suppose what is perhaps true, that the plays of Terence were versions of Menander, nothing translated seems ever to have risen to high reputation. The French, in the meridian hour of their learning, were very laudably industrious to enrich their own language with the wisdom of the ancients, but found themselves reduced, by whatever necessity, to turn the Greek and Roman poetry into prose. Whoever could read an author could translate him. From such rivals little can be feared.

The chief help of Pope in this arduous undertaking was drawn from the versions of Dryden. Virgil had borrowed much of his imagery from Homer, and part of the debt was now paid by his translator. Pope searched the pages of Dryden for happy combinations of heroic diction, but it will not be denied that he added much to what he found. He cultivated our language with so much diligence and art that he has left in his Homer a treasure of poetical elegances to posterity. His version may be said to have tuned the English tongue, for since its appearance no writer, however deficient in other powers, has wanted melody. Such a series of lines so elaborately corrected and so sweetly modulated took possession of the public ear; the vulgar was enamored of the poem, and the learned wondered at the translation.

But in the most general applause discordant voices will always be heard. It has been objected by some, who wish to be numbered among the sons of learning, that Pope's version of Homer is not Homerical; that it exhibits no resemblance of the original and characteristic manner of the father of poetry as it wants[54] his awful simplicity, his artless grandeur, his unaffected majesty. This cannot be totally denied, but it must be remembered that *necessitas quod cogit defendit,* that may be lawfully done which cannot be forborne. Time and place will always enforce regard. In estimating this translation, consideration must be had of the nature of our language, the form of our meter, and, above all, of the change which two thousand years have made in the modes of life and the habits of thought. Virgil wrote in a language of the

[54] Lacks.

same general fabric with that of Homer, in verses of the same measure, and in an age nearer to Homer's time by eighteen hundred years; yet he found even then the state of the world so much altered and the demand for elegance so much increased that mere nature would be endured no longer; and perhaps in the multitude of borrowed passages very few can be shown which he has not embellished.

There is a time when nations emerging from barbarity and falling into regular subordination gain leisure to grow wise and feel the shame of ignorance and the craving pain of unsatisfied curiosity. To this hunger of the mind plain sense is grateful; that which fills the void removes uneasiness, and to be free from pain for a while is pleasure; but repletion generates fastidiousness, a saturated intellect soon becomes luxurious,[55] and knowledge finds no willing reception till it is recommended by artificial diction. Thus it will be found as learning advances that in all nations the first writers are simple and that every age improves in elegance. One refinement always makes way for another, and what was expedient to Virgil was necessary to Pope.

I suppose many readers of the English *Iliad,* when they have been touched with some unexpected beauty of the lighter kind, have tried to enjoy it in the original, where, alas! it was not to be found. Homer doubtless owes to his translator many Ovidian graces not exactly suitable to his character, but to have added can be no great crime if nothing be taken away. Elegance is surely to be desired if it be not gained at the expense of dignity. A hero would wish to be loved as well as to be reverenced.

To a thousand cavils one answer is sufficient: the purpose of a writer is to be read, and the criticism which would destroy the power of pleasing must be blown aside. Pope wrote for his own age and his own nation; he knew that it was necessary to color the images and point the sentiments of his author; he therefore made him graceful but lost him some of his sublimity.

The copious notes with which the version is accompanied and by which it is recommended to many readers, though they were undoubtedly written to swell the volumes, ought not to pass without praise: commentaries which attract the reader by the pleasure of

[55] Excessively refined.

perusal have not often appeared; the notes of others are read to clear difficulties, those of Pope to vary entertainment.

It has, however, been objected with sufficient reason that there is in the commentary too much of unseasonable levity and affected gaiety; that too many appeals are made to the ladies, and the ease which is so carefully preserved is sometimes the ease of a trifler. Every art has its terms and every kind of instruction its proper style; the gravity of common critics may be tedious but is less despicable than childish merriment.

Of the *Odyssey* nothing remains to be observed; the same general praise may be given to both translations, and a particular examination of either would require a large volume. The notes were written by Broome, who endeavored not unsuccessfully to imitate his master.

Of *The Dunciad* the hint is confessedly taken from Dryden's *MacFlecknoe,* but the plan is so enlarged and diversified as justly to claim the praise of an original and affords perhaps the best specimen that has yet appeared of personal satire ludicrously pompous.[56]

That the design was moral, whatever the author might tell either his readers or himself, I am not convinced. The first motive was the desire of revenging the contempt with which Theobald[57] had treated his Shakespeare and regaining the honor which he had lost, by crushing his opponent. Theobald was not of bulk enough to fill a poem, and therefore it was necessary to find other enemies with other names at whose expense he might divert the public.

In this design there was petulance and malignity enough, but I cannot think it very criminal. An author places himself uncalled before the tribunal of criticism and solicits fame at the hazard of disgrace. Dullness or deformity are not culpable in themselves but may be very justly reproached when they pretend to the honor of wit or the influence of beauty. If bad writers were to pass without reprehension, what should restrain them? *impune diem consumpserit ingens Telephus,*[58] and upon bad writers only will censure have much effect. The satire which brought Theobald and Moore into contempt, dropped

---

[56] Comically inflated, mock heroic.

[57] An editor of Shakespeare who had criticized Pope's Shakespeare edition and who was satirized in the first version of *The Dunciad* (1728).

[58] Juvenal's criticism of Euripides's play *Telephus:* "Shall an endless Telephus take a whole day with impunity?"

impotent from Bentley, like the javelin of Priam thrown at Neoptolemus.

All truth is valuable, and satirical criticism may be considered as useful when it rectifies error and improves judgment; he that refines the public taste is a public benefactor.

The beauties of this poem are well known; its chief fault is the grossness of its images. Pope and Swift had an unnatural delight in ideas physically impure such as every other tongue utters with unwillingness and of which every ear shrinks from the mention.

But even this fault, offensive as it is, may be forgiven for the excellence of other passages, such as the formation and dissolution of Moore, the account of the Traveler, the misfortune of the Florist, and the crowded thoughts and stately numbers which dignify the concluding paragraph.

The alterations which have been made in *The Dunciad,* not always for the better, require that it should be published, as in the last collection,[59] with all its variations.

The *Essay on Man* was a work of great labor and long consideration, but certainly not the happiest of Pope's performances. The subject is perhaps not very proper for poetry, and the poet was not sufficiently master of his subject; metaphysical morality was to him a new study, he was proud of his acquisitions, and, supposing himself master of great secrets, was in haste to teach what he had not learned. Thus he tells us in the first Epistle that from the nature of the Supreme Being may be deduced an order of beings such as mankind because infinite excellence can do only what is best. He finds out that "all the question is whether man be in a wrong place." Surely if, according to the poet's Leibnitian reasoning,[60] we may infer that man ought to be only because he is, we may allow that his place is the right place because he has it. Supreme Wisdom is not less infallible in disposing than in creating. But what is meant by *somewhere* and *place* and *wrong place* it had been vain to ask Pope, who probably had never asked himself.

Having exalted himself into the chair of wisdom, he tells us much

[59] Edition.

[60] The philosopher Gottfried Wilhelm Leibniz had argued, in his *Theodicy* (1710), that there is a "pre-established harmony" in the universe, that this is the best possible world, and that everything in it has its proper place.

that every man knows and much that he does not know himself: that we see but little and that the order of the universe is beyond our comprehension, an opinion not very uncommon; and that there is a chain of subordinate beings "from infinite to nothing," of which himself and his readers are equally ignorant. But he gives us one comfort which, without his help, he supposes unattainable, in the position "that though we are fools, yet God is wise."

This *Essay* affords an egregious instance of the predominance of genius, the dazzling splendor of imagery, and the seductive powers of eloquence. Never were penury of knowledge and vulgarity of sentiment[61] so happily disguised. The reader feels his mind full though he learns nothing; and when he meets it in its new array no longer knows the talk of his mother and his nurse. When these wonder-working sounds sink into sense and the doctrine of the *Essay,* disrobed of its ornaments, is left to the powers of its naked excellence, what shall we discover? That we are, in comparison with our Creator, very weak and ignorant; that we do not uphold the chain of existence; and that we could not make one another with more skill than we are made. We may learn yet more: that the arts of human life were copied from the instinctive operations of other animals; that if the world be made for man, it may be said that man was made for geese. To these profound principles of natural knowledge are added some moral instructions equally new: that self-interest, well understood, will produce social concord; that men are mutual gainers by mutual benefits; that evil is sometimes balanced by good; that human advantages are unstable and fallacious, of uncertain duration and doubtful effects; that our true honor is not to have a great part but to act it well; that virtue only is our own; and that happiness is always in our power.

Surely a man of no very comprehensive search may venture to say that he has heard all this before, but it was never till now recommended by such a blaze of embellishment or such sweetness of melody. The vigorous contraction of some thoughts, the luxuriant amplification of others, the incidental illustrations, and sometimes the dignity, sometimes the softness of the verses enchain philosophy, suspend criticism, and oppress judgment by overpowering pleasure.

This is true of many paragraphs; yet if I had undertaken to exemplify Pope's felicity of composition before a rigid critic, I should

---

[61] Undistinguished, commonplace ideas.

not select the *Essay on Man,* for it contains more lines unsuccessfully labored, more harshness of diction, more thoughts imperfectly expressed, more levity without elegance, and more heaviness without strength than will easily be found in all his other works. . . .[62]

Pope had, in proportions very nicely adjusted to each other, all the qualities that constitute genius. He had *invention*, by which new trains of events are formed and new scenes of imagery displayed, as in *The Rape of the Lock*, or extrinsic and adventitious embellishments and illustrations are connected with a known subject, as in the *Essay on Criticism*. He had *imagination*, which strongly impresses on the writer's mind and enables him to convey to the reader the various forms of nature, incidents of life, and energies of passion, as in his *Eloisa, Windsor Forest,* and the *Ethic Epistles*. He had *judgment*, which selects from life or nature what the present purpose requires, and by separating the essence of things from its concomitants often makes the representation more powerful than the reality; and he had colors of language always before him, ready to decorate his matter with every grace of elegant expression, as when he accommodates his diction to the wonderful multiplicity of Homer's sentiments and descriptions.

Poetical expression includes sound as well as meaning. "Music," says Dryden, "is inarticulate poetry"; among the excellences of Pope, therefore, must be mentioned the melody of his meter. By perusing the works of Dryden, he discovered the most perfect fabric of English verse and habituated himself to that only which he found the best, in consequence of which restraint his poetry has been censured as too uniformly musical and as glutting the ear with unvaried sweetness. I suspect this objection to be the cant[63] of those who judge by principles rather than perception and who would even themselves have less pleasure in his works if he had tried to relieve attention by studied discords or affected to break his lines and vary his pauses.

But though he was thus careful of his versification, he did not oppress his powers with superfluous rigor. He seems to have thought with Boileau that the practice of writing might be refined till the difficulty should overbalance the advantage. The construction of his lan-

---

[62] Brief discussions of the *Moral Essays, Epistle to Dr. Arbuthnot,* and other late poems are omitted.

[63] Jargon.

guage is not always strictly grammatical; with those rhymes which prescription had conjoined he contented himself, without regard to Swift's remonstrances, though there was no striking consonance; nor was he very careful to vary his terminations or to refuse admission at a small distance to the same rhymes. . . .

New sentiments and new images others may produce, but to attempt any further improvement of versification will be dangerous. Art and diligence have now done their best, and what shall be added will be the effort of tedious toil and needless curiosity.

After all this it is surely superfluous to answer the question that has once been asked, whether Pope was a poet? otherwise than by asking in return, if Pope be not a poet, where is poetry to be found? To circumscribe poetry by a definition will only show the narrowness of the definer, though a definition which shall exclude Pope will not easily be made. Let us look round upon the present time and back upon the past; let us inquire to whom the voice of mankind has decreed the wreath of poetry; let their productions be examined and their claims stated, and the pretensions of Pope will be no more disputed. Had he given the world only his version the name of poet must have been allowed him; if the writer of the *Iliad* were to class his successors, he would assign a very high place to his translator without requiring any other evidence of genius.

GRAY

Gray's poetry is now to be considered, and I hope not to be looked on as an enemy to his name if I confess that I contemplate it with less pleasure than his life.

His ode on *Spring* has something poetical, both in the language and the thought, but the language is too luxuriant and the thoughts have nothing new. There has of late arisen a practice of giving to adjectives derived from substantives the termination of participles, such as the *cultured* plain, the *daisied* bank, but I was sorry to see in the lines of a scholar like Gray the *honied* Spring. The morality is natural but too stale; the conclusion is pretty.

The poem on the *Cat* was doubtless by its author considered as a trifle, but it is not a happy trifle. In the first stanza "the azure flowers" that "blow" show resolutely a rhyme is sometimes made when it cannot easily be found. Selima, the *cat*, is called a nymph, with some violence both to language and sense, but there is [no] good use made of it when it is done; for of the two lines,

> What female heart can gold despise?
> What cat's averse to fish?

the first relates merely to the nymph and the second only to the cat. The sixth stanza contains a melancholy truth, that "a favorite has no friend"; but the last ends in a pointed sentence[64] of no relation to the purpose: if "what glistered" had been "gold," the cat would not have gone into the water; and if she had, would not less have been drowned.

The *Prospect of Eton College* suggests nothing to Gray which every beholder does not equally think and feel. His supplication to Father Thames to tell him who drives the hoop or tosses the ball is useless and puerile. Father Thames has no better means of knowing than himself. His epithet "buxom health" is not elegant; he seems not to understand the word. Gray thought his language more poetical as it was more remote from common use; finding in Dryden "honey redolent of spring," an expression that reaches the utmost limits of our language, Gray drove it a little more beyond common apprehension by making "gales" to be "redolent of joy and youth."

Of the *Ode on Adversity*, the hint was at first taken from *O Diva, gratum quæ regis Antium,*[65] but Gray has excelled his original by the variety of his sentiments and by their moral application. Of this piece, at once poetical and rational, I will not by slight objections violate the dignity.

My process has now brought me to the "wonderful wonder of wonders," the two sister odes,[66] by which, though either vulgar ignorance or common sense at first universally rejected them, many have

---

[64] Witty point or maxim.

[65] Horace, *Odes,* I, xxxv, 1. 1: "Goddess, who rulest thy loved Antium."

[66] The Pindaric odes: *The Progress of Poetry* and *The Bard.*

been since persuaded to think themselves delighted. I am one of those that are willing to be pleased and therefore would gladly find the meaning of the first stanza of the *Progress of Poetry*.

Gray seems in his rapture to confound the images of "spreading sound" and "running water." A "stream of music" may be allowed; but where does music, however "smooth and strong," after having visited the "verdant vales," "rowl down the steep amain," so as that "rocks and nodding groves rebellow to the roar"? If this be said of *music*, it is nonsense; if it be said of *water*, it is nothing to the purpose.

The second stanza, exhibiting Mars's car and Jove's eagle, is unworthy of further notice. Criticism disdains to chase a schoolboy to his commonplaces.

To the third it may likewise be objected that it is drawn from mythology, though such as may be more easily assimilated to real life. Idalia's "velvet-green" has something of cant.[67] An epithet or metaphor drawn from nature ennobles art; and epithet or metaphor drawn from art degrades nature. Gray is too fond of words arbitrarily compounded. "Many-twinkling" was formerly censured as not analogical;[68] we may say "many-spotted" but scarcely "many-spotting." This stanza, however, has something pleasing.

Of the second ternary[69] of stanzas, the first endeavors to tell something and would have told it had it not been crossed by Hyperion; the second describes well enough the universal prevalence of poetry; but I am afraid that the conclusion will not rise from the premises. The caverns of the North and the plains of Chile are not the residences of "glory" and "generous shame." But that poetry and virtue go always together is an opinion so pleasing that I can forgive him who resolves to think it true.

The third stanza sounds big with "Delphi," and "Aegean," and "Ilissus," and "Meander," and "hallowed fountain," and "solemn sound"; but in all Gray's odes there is a kind of cumbrous splendor which we wish away. His position is at last false: in the time of Dante

---

67 Inappropriate language.

68 Similar to known grammatical forms.

69 Triad, group of three related stanzas.

and Petrarch, from whom he derives our first school of poetry, Italy was overrun by "tyrant power" and "coward vice," nor was our state much better when we first borrowed the Italian arts.

Of the third ternary, the first gives a mythological birth of Shakespeare. What is said of that mighty genius is true, but it is not said happily; the real effects of his poetical power are put out of sight by the pomp of machinery. Where truth is sufficient to fill the mind, fiction is worse than useless; the counterfeit debases the genuine.

His account of Milton's blindness, if we suppose it caused by study in the formation of his poem—a supposition surely allowable—is poetically true and happily imagined. But the "car" of Dryden with his "two coursers" has nothing in it peculiar; it is a car in which any other rider may be placed.

The Bard appears at the first view to be, as Algarotti and others have remarked, an imitation of the prophecy of Nereus.[70] Algarotti thinks it superior to its original, and if preference depends only on the imagery and animation of the two poems, his judgment is right. There is in *The Bard* more force, more thought, and more variety. But to copy is less than to invent, and the copy has been unhappily produced at a wrong time. The fiction of Horace was to the Romans credible, but its revival disgusts as with apparent and unconquerable falsehood. *Incredulus odi.*[71]

To select a singular event and swell it to a giant's bulk by fabulous appendages of specters and predictions has little difficulty, for he that forsakes the probable may always find the marvelous; and it has little use: we are affected only as we believe; we are improved only as we find something to be imitated or declined. I do not see that *The Bard* promotes any truth, moral or political.

His stanzas are too long, especially his epodes[72]; the ode is finished before the ear has learned its measures and consequently before it can receive pleasure from their consonance and recurrence.

Of the first stanza the abrupt beginning has been celebrated, but technical beauties can give praise only to the inventor. It is in the

---

[70] In Horace's *Odes,* I, xv.

[71] Horace, *Art of Poetry,* 188: "I disbelieve and despise."

[72] Third stanza of the three-part units characteristic of Pindaric odes.

power of any man to rush abruptly upon his subject that has read the ballad of *Johnny Armstrong*:

> Is there ever a man in all Scotland—

The initial resemblances or alliterations, "ruin," "ruthless," "helm nor hauberk," are below the grandeur of a poem that endeavors at sublimity.

In the second stanza the *Bard* is well described, but in the third we have the puerilities of obsolete mythology. When we are told that "Cadwallo hushed the stormy main," and that "Modred" made "huge Plinlimmon bow his cloud-topped head," attention recoils from the repetition of a tale that even when it was first heard was heard with scorn.

The "weaving" of the "winding sheet" he borrowed, as he owns, from the Northern bards, but their texture, however, was very properly the work of female powers, as the act of spinning the thread of life in another mythology. Theft is always dangerous; Gray has made weavers of his slaughtered bards by a fiction outrageous and incongruous. They are then called upon to "weave the warp, and weave the woof," perhaps with no great propriety, for it is by crossing the "woof" with the "warp" that men "weave" the "web" or piece; and the first line was dearly bought by the admission of its wretched correspondent, "Give ample room and verge enough." He has, however, no other line as bad.

The third stanza of the second ternary is commended, I think, beyond its merit. The personification is indistinct. *Thirst* and *Hunger* are not alike; and their features, to make the imagery perfect, should have been discriminated. We are told in the same stanza how "towers" are "fed." But I will no longer look for particular faults; yet let it be observed that the ode might have been concluded with an action of better example, but suicide is always to be had without expense of thought.

These odes are marked by glittering accumulations of ungraceful ornaments; they strike rather than please; the images are magnified by affectation; the language is labored into harshness. The mind of the writer seems to work with unnatural violence. "Double, double, toil and trouble."[73] He has a kind of strutting dignity and is tall by walking on tiptoe. His art and his struggle are too visible, and there is too little appearance of ease and nature.

To say that he has no beauties would be unjust; a man like him, of great learning and great industry, could not but produce something valuable. When he pleases least, it can only be said that a good design was ill directed.

His translations of Northern and Welsh poetry deserve praise; the imagery is preserved, perhaps often improved; but the language is unlike the language of other poets.

In the character of his Elegy I rejoice to concur with the common reader; for by the common sense of readers uncorrupted with literary prejudices, after all the refinements of subtilty and the dogmatism of learning, must be finally decided all claim to poetical honors. The *Churchyard* abounds with images which find a mirror in every mind and with sentiments to which every bosom returns an echo. The four stanzas beginning "Yet even these bones" are to me original: I have never seen the notions in any other place; yet he that reads them here persuades himself that he has always felt them. Had Gray written often thus, it had been vain to blame and useless to praise him.

---

[73] A mocking quotation from the witches' chant in *Macbeth,* IV, i.

5

BOSWELL'S *LIFE OF JOHNSON* (1791)

Johnson . . . did not refrain from expressing himself concerning that nobleman [the Earl of Chesterfield[1]] with pointed freedom: "This man (said he) I thought to be a lord among wits, but, I find, he is only a wit among lords!" And when his *Letters* to his natural son were published, he observed that "they teach the morals of a whore and the manners of a dancing master." (*1754*)

At this time the controversy concerning the pieces published by Mr. James Macpherson as translations of *Ossian*[2] was at its height. Johnson had all along denied their authenticity, and what was still more provoking to their admirers, maintained that they had no merit. . . . Dr. Blair, relying on the internal evidence of their antiquity, asked Dr. Johnson whether he thought any man of a modern age could have written such poems. Johnson replied: "Yes, Sir, many men, many women, and many children." (*1763*)

Rousseau's treatise on the inequality of mankind was at this time a fashionable topic. It gave rise to an observation by Mr. Dempster

---

[1] The Earl of Chesterfield had disappointed Johnson by ignoring his appeal for financial support for the *Dictionary*. The Earl's *Letters to his Son* give worldly advice to his illegitimate son on how to behave in society.

[2] A primitive Celtic bard whose poems were supposedly found but actually composed by Macpherson.

that the advantages of fortune and rank were nothing to a wise man, who ought to value only merit. JOHNSON: "If man were a savage, living in the woods by himself, this might be true, but in civilized society we all depend upon each other and our happiness is very much owing to the good opinion of mankind. Now, Sir, in civilized society, external advantages make us more respected. A man with a good coat upon his back meets with a better reception than he who has a bad one. Sir, you may analyze this and say what is there in it? But that will avail you nothing, for it is part of a general system. Pound St. Paul's Church into atoms and consider any single atom; it is, to be sure, good for nothing; but put all these atoms together and you have St. Paul's Church. So it is with human felicity, which is made up of many ingredients, each of which may be shown to be very insignificant. In civilized society, personal merit will not serve you as well as money will. . . . He who is rich in a civilized society must be happier than he who is poor, as riches, if properly used (and it is a man's own fault if they are not) must be productive of the highest advantages. Money, to be sure, of itself is of no use, for its only use is to part with it. Rousseau and all those who deal in paradoxes are led away by a childish desire of novelty." (*1763*)

I told him that Voltaire, in a conversation with me, had distinguished Pope and Dryden thus: "Pope drives a handsome chariot with a couple of neat trim nags; Dryden a coach and six stately horses." JOHNSON: "Why, Sir, the truth is, they both drive coaches and six; but Dryden's horses are either galloping or stumbling, Pope's go at a steady even trot." (*1766*)

Johnson said (sarcastically): "It seems, Sir, you have kept very good company abroad. . . ." [I] answered with a smile: "My dear Sir, you don't call Rousseau bad company. Do you really think *him* a bad man?" JOHNSON: "Sir, if you are talking jestingly of this, I don't talk with you. If you mean to be serious, I think him one of the worst of men; a rascal who ought to be hunted out of society, as he has been. Three or four nations have expelled him, and it is a shame that he is protected in this country."[3] BOSWELL: "I don't deny, Sir, but that his

[3] Rousseau had temporarily taken refuge in England after being expelled from France and Switzerland for his unorthodox ideas.

novel may perhaps do harm, but I cannot think his intention was bad." JOHNSON: "Sir, that will not do. We cannot prove any man's intention to be bad. You may shoot a man through the head and say you intended to miss him, but the judge will order you to be hanged. An alleged want of intention when evil is committed will not be allowed in a court of justice. Rousseau, Sir, is a very bad man. I would sooner sign a sentence for his transportation than that of any felon who has gone from the Old Bailey these many years. Yes, I should like to have him work in the plantations." BOSWELL: "Sir, do you think him as bad a man as Voltaire?"[4] JOHNSON: "Why, Sir, it is difficult to settle the proportion of iniquity between them." (*1766*)

"Sir, . . . there is all the difference in the world between characters of nature and characters of manners,[5] and *there* is the difference between the characters of Fielding and those of Richardson. Characters of manners are very entertaining, but they are to be understood by a more superficial observer than characters of nature, where a man must dive into the recesses of the human heart."

In comparing those two writers [Richardson and Fielding], he used this expression: "that there was as great a difference between them as between a man who knew how a watch was made, and a man who could tell the hour by looking on the dial-plate." (*1768*)

I attempted to argue for the superior happiness of the savage life. . . . JOHNSON: "Sir, there can be nothing more false. The savages have no bodily advantages beyond those of civilized men. They have not better health; and as to care and mental uneasiness, they are not above it but below it, like bears. No, Sir, you are not to talk such paradox; let me have no more on't. It cannot entertain, far less can it instruct. Lord Monboddo, one of your Scotch judges, talked a great deal of such nonsense.[6] I suffered *him*, but I will not suffer *you*." BOSWELL: "But, Sir, does not Rousseau talk such nonsense?" JOHNSON: "True, Sir, but Rousseau *knows* he is talking nonsense, and laughs at the world for staring at him." BOSWELL: "How so, Sir?" JOHNSON: "Why, Sir, a

---

[4] Voltaire was notorious for his anti-religious and otherwise iconoclastic views.

[5] See Introduction and chapter 3, n. 25.

[6] James Burnett, Lord Monboddo, was already known for his belief that human beings were healthier and more virtuous in a primitive state than in society. His *Origin and Progress of Language* began to appear in 1773.

man who talks nonsense so well must know that he is talking nonsense." (*1769*)

After dinner our conversation first turned upon Pope. Johnson said his characters of men were admirably drawn, those of women not so well. He repeated to us in his forcible melodious manner the concluding lines of the *Dunciad*. While he was talking loudly in praise of those lines, one of the company ventured to say, "Too fine for such a poem—a poem on what?" JOHNSON (with a disdainful look): "Why, on *dunces*. It was worth while being a dunce then. Ah, Sir, Hadst *thou* lived in those days! It is not worth while being a dunce now, when there are no wits." (*1769*)

Speaking of the French novels compared with Richardson's, he said they might be pretty baubles but a wren was not an eagle. (*1770*)

Fielding being mentioned, Johnson exclaimed, "He was a blockhead"; and upon my expressing my astonishment at so strange an assertion, he said, "What I mean by his being a blockhead is that he was a barren rascal." BOSWELL: "Will you not allow, Sir, that he draws very natural pictures of human life?" JOHNSON: "Why, Sir, it is of very low life. Richardson used to say that had he not known who Fielding was, he should have believed he was an ostler.[7] Sir, there is more knowledge of the human heart in one letter of Richardson's[8] than in all *Tom Jones*. I, indeed, never read *Joseph Andrews*." ERSKINE: "Surely, Sir, Richardson is very tedious." JOHNSON: "Why, Sir, if you were to read Richardson for the story, your impatience would be so much fretted that you would hang yourself. But you must read him for the sentiment and consider the story as only giving occasion to the sentiment." (*1772*)

Dr. Goldsmith's new play, *She Stoops to Conquer,* being mentioned: JOHNSON: "I know of no comedy for many years that has so much exhilarated an audience, that has answered so much the great end of comedy—making an audience merry." (*1773*)

---

[7] Groom, stableman.

[8] Samuel Richardson's novels were written in letter form.

Johnson praised John Bunyan highly. "His *Pilgrim's Progress* has great merit, both for invention, imagination, and the conduct of the story; and it has had the best evidence of its merit, the general and continued approbation of mankind. Few books, I believe, have had a more extensive sale." (*1773*)

I mentioned Sir Richard Steele having published his *Christian Hero* with the avowed purpose of obliging himself to lead a religious life, yet that his conduct was by no means strictly suitable. JOHNSON: "Steele, I believe, practised the lighter vices." (*1776*)

"Nothing odd will do long. *Tristram Shandy* did not last." (*1776*)

I have already mentioned that Johnson was very desirous of reconciliation with old Mr. Sheridan. It will, therefore, not seem at all surprising that he was zealous in acknowledging the brilliant merit of his son.[9] While it had as yet been displayed only in the drama, Johnson proposed him as a member of The Literary Club, observing that "He who has written the two best comedies of his age is surely a considerable man." (*1777*)

Talking of Gray's *Odes,* he said, "They are forced plants raised in a hot-bed, and they are poor plants; they are but cucumbers after all." A gentleman present, who had been running down ode-writing in general as a bad species of poetry, unluckily said, "Had they been literally cucumbers, they had been better things than odes."—"Yes, Sir, (said Johnson) for a *hog*." (*1780*)

Mrs. Kennicot related . . . a lively saying of Dr. Johnson to Miss Hannah More, who had expressed a wonder that the poet who had written *Paradise Lost* should write such poor sonnets: "Milton, Madam, was a genius that could cut a Colossus from a rock but could not carve heads upon cherry-stones." (*1784*)

---

[9] Richard Brinsley Sheridan, author of the comedies *The Rivals* (1775) and *The School for Scandal* (1777). His father, Thomas Sheridan, a well-known lecturer on elocution, educator, and former theater manager, was estranged from Johnson because of a cutting remark of Johnson's.

BIBLIOGRAPHY

Modern Collected Editions

The Yale Edition of the Works of Samuel Johnson. New Haven, 1958–date. (Includes *The Idler and the Adventurer,* ed. W. J. Bate, John M. Bullitt, L. F. Powell, 1963; *Johnson on Shakespeare,* ed. Arthur Sherbo, 2 vols., 1968; *The Rambler,* ed. W. J. Bate and Albrecht B. Strauss, 3 vols., 1969. Other volumes are in progress.)

Lives of the English Poets, ed. George Birkbeck Hill. 3 vols. Oxford, 1905; repr. 1968.

Works About Johnson

Bate, Walter Jackson. *Samuel Johnson.* New York, 1977.

Booth, Mark W. "Johnson's Critical Judgments in the *Lives of the Poets.*" *SEL* 16 (1976): 505–15.

Boswell's Life of Johnson, ed. Chauncey Brewster Tinker. 2 vols. New York, 1933.

Boulton, James T., ed. *Johnson: The Critical Heritage.* New York, 1971.

Bronson, Bertrand H. Introduction. *Johnson on Shakespeare,* ed. Arthur Sherbo. Vol. I. New Haven, 1968.

Chapin, Chester F. *The Religious Thought of Samuel Johnson.* Ann Arbor, 1968.

Damrosch, Leopold, Jr. *The Uses of Johnson's Criticism.* Charlottesville, 1976.

Edinger, William. *Samuel Johnson and Poetic Style.* Chicago, 1977.

Eliot, T. S. "Johnson as Critic and Poet." *On Poetry and Poets*. London, 1957.

Fussell, Paul. *Samuel Johnson and the Life of Writing*. New York, 1971.

Greene, Donald J. *Samuel Johnson*. New York, 1970.

Hagstrum, Jean H. *Samuel Johnson's Literary Criticism*. Minneapolis, 1952.

Keast, W. R. "The Theoretical Foundations of Johnson's Criticism." In *Critics and Criticism, Ancient and Modern,* ed. R. S. Crane. Chicago, 1952.

Krieger, Murray. "Fiction, Nature, and Literary Kinds in Johnson's Criticism of Shakespeare." *Eighteenth Century Studies* 4 (1971): 184–98.

Leavis, F. R. "Johnson as Critic." *Scrutiny* 12 (1944): 187–204; repr. in *Samuel Johnson: A Collection of Critical Essays,* ed. Donald J. Greene. Englewood, 1965.

Stock, Robert D. *Samuel Johnson and Neoclassical Dramatic Theory: The Intellectual Context of the Preface to Shakespeare*. Lincoln, Neb., 1973.

Wain, John. Introduction. *Johnson as Critic*. London, 1973.

————. *Samuel Johnson*. New York, 1974.

Wellek, Rene. "Dr. Johnson." *A History of Modern Criticism: 1750–1950*. Vol. I. New Haven, 1955.

Wimsatt, W. K., Jr. Introduction. *Samuel Johnson on Shakespeare*. New York, 1960.

————, and Cleanth Brooks. "The Neo-Classical Universal: Samuel Johnson." *Literary Criticism: A Short History*. New York, 1957.